HUTCHINSON

Quiz Link

HUTCHINSON

Quiz Link

BILL MURRAY

Helicon

Copyright © Helicon Publishing Ltd 1995
Reprinted 1998

All rights reserved

Helicon Publishing Ltd
42 Hythe Bridge Street
Oxford OX1 2EP
e-mail: admin@helicon.co.uk
Website: http://www.helicon.co.uk

ISBN 1-85986-145-8

British Cataloguing in Publication Data
A catalogue record for this book is available from the
British Library

Typeset by TechType, Abingdon, Oxon
Printed and bound in Denmark by
Nørhaven A/S, Viborg

Introduction

Welcome to The *Hutchinson Quizlink* quizbook. This is a new type of quizbook where you not only have to answer the questions, you also have to work out what links the answers together.

Each set of questions constitutes one round, and the answers to each set of questions contain a link of some kind. This link, the quizlink, could be a word or words, or the names of people. It may be something very straightforward and immediately obvious, or something a little more devious.

A typical round would be:

1 Which singer had a number 1 hit in 1974 with a song called 'Gonna Make You A Star'?
2 What was the alias used by Superman while working as a reporter for the *Daily Planet* newspaper?
3 Which English actress played the part of Fleur in the television production of John Galsworthy's *The Forsythe Saga*?
4 Which bowler took nine wickets in an innings for the England cricket team in a test match against South Africa in 1994?
5 Which British author wrote the novel *Of Human Bondage*?

The answers are as follows:
1 David ESSEX
2 Clark KENT
3 Susan HAMPSHIRE
4 DEVON Malcolm
5 SOMERSET Maugham

      Quizlink = Names of English COUNTIES

As you see, the link between the answers is that they all contain the name of an English county. Easy, isn't it? This example may be, but be warned! They are not all such giveaways.

How to use the book

Quizlink has been specially devised for team play – but can be used in any way you like.

How to play the game

To play the game you will need somebody to act as quizmaster. It is possible to do this yourself if there are only two people playing, but it will be very difficult to avoid seeing the answers to future questions when looking for the answer you want. You will probably find it useful to have a pen and paper to keep a note of the answers when trying to identify the link.

Each game consists of six complete rounds. Teams should consist of an equal number of players on each side. The teams should toss a coin to decide who will receive the first question. The team winning the toss will then select a number corresponding to one of the question numbers in Round 1. The quiz master will read the question from the book and the team answering (Team A) will be given 30 seconds to provide an answer.

If they answer correctly they are awarded two points and are given an opportunity to identify the quizlink (what it is that links the answers together). Should they successfully identify the link they are awarded a further three points.

A team shall be deemed to have correctly identified the link if their answer contains the keyword given in the quizlink.

The keyword is the word or words given in capital letters after the = sign. In the example given earlier (Quizlink = Names of English COUNTIES) the keyword is COUNTIES.

Should Team A be unable to answer the original question however, it should be passed to their opponents (Team B) who will be given a further 15 seconds to provide a correct answer for a one-point bonus. A correct answer will entitle them to an attempt at identifying the quizlink. Once again three points are awarded for a successful identification.

If both teams are unable to answer the original question correctly, the quizmaster should NOT divulge the answer, as these questions will be returned to after the link has been identified. If, after the link has been identified, and a question has been asked to both teams a second time and they are still unable to answer, the quizmaster can then reveal the answer.

Team B should then select a number corresponding to one of the unanswered questions from Round 1, and the same procedure as for the previous question is followed. In all cases an attempt at identifying the quizlink will only be awarded after a team has given a correct answer to a question.

The same pattern is followed for the remaining questions in Round 1. If and when the link is identified, the remaining questions should still be asked to the teams in turn, and the scoring system of two points or one bonus point maintained. This is to ensure that each team receives the same number of questions. It also makes the questions a little easier to answer, as you already know the link. The answer to the question 'Who wrote *The Dong With The Luminous Nose* ?' may not be blindingly obvious at first, but if you know that all the answers contain the name of a Shakespearean king then you may be able to deduce that the correct answer is Edward Lear.

If both teams are unable to identify the link after all questions have been asked, the quizmaster should reveal the link to both teams and return to the remaining questions in team order.

Round 2 begins with Team B selecting a number corresponding to one of the question numbers available and proceeds as Round 1 until all questions have been asked. Rounds 3–6 follow the same pattern and the team with most points after Round 6 is of course the winner.

The book contains 30 complete games of six rounds each.

Have fun.
Bill Murray

Thanks to Tony for the help and inspiration.

Game 1 — Rounds 1–3

Round 1
1. Which mountain was believed by the ancient Greeks to be the source of poetic inspiration and home of the Muses?
2. Which character did Nerys Hughes play in the television comedy show *The Liver Birds*?
3. Who remained in the command module when Armstrong and Aldrin became the first men to walk on the Moon in 1969?
4. Which British prime minister assumed the title Earl of Stockton?
5. Which villain did Danny de Vito play in the 1992 film *Batman Returns*?

Round 2
1. Who was Peter Bowles' co-star in the television series *Perfect Scoundrels*?
2. What was the name of the Venetian traveller who visited Kublai Khan in the 13th century?
3. In an industrial context, for what are the initials ICI an abbreviation?
4. What type of weapon was the Zulu assegai?
5. Angie Dickinson starred in the title role in the television drama *Police Woman*. What was the name of the character she portrayed?

Round 3
1. What name is given to a garden shack which is generally used as a store for tools and seedlings?
2. The list of the 92 naturally occurring chemical elements arranged according to their atomic numbers is known as what?
3. What was dismantled and reassembled in Arizona in the USA during the 1960s?
4. Who was the original lead vocalist with rock band Led Zeppelin?
5. What was the title of Ronald Reagan's 1991 autobiography?

Game 1 — Rounds 1–3

Round 1
1. HELICON
2. Sandra HUTCHINSON
3. Michael COLLINS
4. Harold MACMILLAN
5. The PENGUIN

        Quizlink = Names of
            PUBLISHERS

Round 2
1. Bryan MURRAY
2. Marco POLO
3. IMPERIAL Chemical Industries
4. It was a kind of SPEAR
5. PEPPER Anderson

        Quizlink = Types of MINTS

Round 3
1. POTTING Shed
2. The Periodic TABLE
3. London BRIDGE
4. Robert PLANT
5. *Where's The REST Of Me?*

        Quizlink = Terms used in SNOOKER
           (accept billiards or pool)

Game 1 — Rounds 4–6

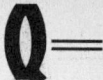

Round 4
1 Who became the 41st president of the USA?
2 Which well-known fictional detective was created by the novelist Dashiell Hammett?
3 Where, according to tradition, was Sir Francis Drake playing bowls when he was warned of the impending invasion of the Spanish Armada?
4 What name is given to the process by which the world's atmosphere is becoming continually warmer?
5 Who was the Wolverhampton Wanderers footballer who made 49 appearances for England between the years of 1955 and 1966?

Round 5
1 What was the nickname given to King Edward I of England?
2 What is the name of Deirdre's daughter in the TV soap *Coronation Street*?
3 Which English general was killed on the Plains of Abraham in 1759?
4 Which world boxing champion forced Muhammad Ali to retire after the tenth round of their fight in 1980?
5 In the US television show *Dynasty*, who was the first husband of Alexis Colby?

Round 6
1 Who played the part of Chief Inspector Barlow in the television show *Softly, Softly*?
2 There are two varieties of artichoke. One of them is called the Jerusalem artichoke; what is the name of the other?
3 Which English humorist is remembered for his *Book of Nonsense* which popularized the limerick?
4 What was the name of the bank manager's secretary in the television comedy show *The Beverly Hillbillies*?
5 What was the title of the second Top 10 hit for the group Dire Straits; the song reaching number 8 in the charts in 1981?

Game 1 — Rounds 4–6

Round 4
1. George BUSH
2. Sam SPADE
3. Plymouth HOE
4. GREENHOUSE Effect
5. Ron FLOWERS

   Quizlink = Things you might find in a GARDEN

Round 5
1. The HAMMER of the Scots
2. TRACY
3. James WOLFE
4. Larry HOLMES
5. BLAKE Carrington

   Quizlink = Surnames of fictional DETECTIVES (Mike Hammer; Dick Tracy; Nero Wolfe; Sherlock Holmes; Sexton Blake)

Round 6
1. STRATFORD Johns
2. The GLOBE artichoke
3. Edward LEAR
4. Miss Jane HATHAWAY
5. 'ROMEO AND JULIET'

   Quizlink = WILLIAM SHAKESPEARE (Stratford-upon-Avon; the Globe Theatre; King Lear; Anne Hathaway)

Game 2 — Rounds 1–3

Round 1
1. Which Elizabethan hero was executed in 1618?
2. Who played the role of Samantha Stevens in the television comedy show *Bewitched*?
3. Who was nicknamed 'the Iron Chancellor'?
4. Which fantastic bird is said to have risen from its own ashes?
5. What was the name of the character played by Walter Matthau in the film *The Odd Couple*?

Round 2
1. Who was the lead singer with the pop group Slade?
2. What was the nickname of jazz musician Charles Christopher Parker?
3. In which county is the port of Southampton?
4. What name is given to the areas in both New York and London that are frequented by musicians?
5. Which character was created by Len Deighton and played in a series of films by Michael Caine?

Round 3
1. What is the title of undoubtedly the most famous painting by Frans Hals?
2. What do astronomers call an exploding star?
3. What is the name of the satellite used by Sky Television?
4. In which film does Marlon Brando become president of Mexico?
5. Who is credited with the invention of the parking meter; the first ones being used in Oklahoma in 1935?

Game 2 — Rounds 1–3

Round 1
1. Sir Walter RALEIGH
2. Elizabeth MONTGOMERY
3. Otto BISMARCK
4. The PHOENIX
5. Oscar MADISON

   Quizlink = US STATE CAPITALS (Raleigh, North Carolina; Montgomery, Alabama; Bismarck, North Dakota; Phoenix, Arizona; Madison, Wisconsin)

Round 2
1. Noddy HOLDER
2. 'BIRD'
3. HAMPSHIRE
4. Tin Pan ALLEY
5. Harry PALMER

   Quizlink = Surnames of first-class cricket UMPIRES (John Holder; Dickie Bird; John Hampshire; Bill Alley; Ken Palmer)

Round 3
1. *The Laughing CAVALIER*
2. A superNOVA
3. *ASTRA*
4. *VIVA Zapata*
5. CARLTON Magee

   Quizlink = Models of VAUXHALL CARS

Game 2 — Rounds 4-6

Round 4
1. What is the correct name of the building which is usually referred to as the Houses of Parliament?
2. Which football club defeated Leeds United in a replay to win the 1970 FA Cup?
3. Who wrote the book *Call of the Wild*?
4. What is the traditional venue for the Promenade concerts?
5. Which famous battle was fought in the year 1815?

Round 5
1. Who succeeded Neil Kinnock as leader of the Labour Party?
2. What was the popular name of the Locomotives and Highways Act passed by parliament in 1865?
3. Which famous scientist formulated the theory of relativity?
4. Which historical conflict occurred on 21 Oct 1805?
5. Which football team were beaten in the FA Cup final three times during the 1960s?

Round 6
1. What name is given to a mound of rough stones set up as a monument or landmark?
2. Who was the founder of the Quaker religion?
3. Which stretch of water lies between Liverpool and the Isle of Man?
4. What is the name of the foodstuff made from a batter of milk, eggs, and flour that is traditionally served with roast beef?
5. On which island off the British coast is Portree the major town?

Game 2 — Rounds 4–6

Round 4
1. The Palace of WESTMINSTER
2. CHELSEA
3. Jack LONDON
4. The Royal ALBERT Hall
5. The Battle of WATERLOO

   Quizlink = BRIDGES over the River Thames

Round 5
1. John SMITH
2. RED Flag Act
3. ALBERT Einstein
4. The Battle of TRAFALGAR
5. LEICESTER City

   Quizlink = Names of well-known SQUARES

Round 6
1. A CAIRN
2. George FOX
3. IRISH Sea
4. YORKSHIRE pudding
5. SKYE

   Quizlink = Breeds of TERRIER

Game 3 — Rounds 1–3

Round 1
1 What was the name of the cartoonist who was well known for his drawings of complex machinery designed to perform everyday tasks?
2 Who was the brother of singer Peter Sarstedt who had a number 1 hit in the British charts with a song called 'Well I Ask You'?
3 According to David Bowie's 'Space Oddity', who were ground control attempting to contact?
4 Which Arsenal and Scotland goalkeeper became a television presenter?
5 In the book *The Adventures of Tom Sawyer* by Mark Twain, what was the name of Tom's sweetheart?

Round 2
1 Which television programme with a sporting connection is presented by David Baddiel and Frank Skinner?
2 Who is the longest-reigning occupant of the British throne?
3 For which book was Kingsley Amis awarded the 1986 Booker Prize?
4 Of what is the majority of the Great Barrier Reef composed?
5 In which book by Charles Dickens does the character Scrooge appear?

Round 3
1 What is the name of the cartoon cat created by Jim Davis?
2 Who wrote *The Shining* and *Misery*?
3 Who plays the part of Curly Watts in *Coronation Street*?
4 Which horse race completes the so-called Spring Double along with the Grand National?
5 Which Irish dramatist wrote the play *Waiting For Godot*?

Game 3 — Rounds 1–3

Round 1
1 HEATH Robinson
2 EDEN Kane
3 MAJOR Tom
4 Bob WILSON
5 Becky THATCHER

Quizlink = Surnames of
British PRIME MINISTERS

Round 2
1 *FANTASY Football League*
2 Queen VICTORIA
3 *The Old DEVILS*
4 CORAL
5 *A CHRISTMAS Carol*

Quizlink = Names of ISLANDS

Round 3
1 GARFIELD
2 Stephen KING
3 Kevin KENNEDY
4 LINCOLN Handicap
5 Samuel BECKET

Quizlink = Surnames of people who were ASSASSINATED
(James Garfield; Martin Luther King; John F and Robert
Kennedy; Abraham Lincoln; Thomas à Becket)

Game 3 — Rounds 4–6

Round 4
1 Which US general planned Operation Desert Storm in 1991?
2 Who played the title role in the 1971 film *Klute*?
3 What is the capital city of the Dominican Republic?
4 Which Scottish physician discovered that citrus fruits could cure and prevent scurvy?
5 Which female singer with the group Bucks Fizz later became a television presenter?

Round 5
1 What was the name of Han Solo's spaceship in the film *Star Wars*?
2 In which television quiz show hosted by Paul Daniels did three couples compete in an attempt to win more time than the others?
3 What was the title of the first winning song sung by Irishman Johnny Logan in the Eurovision Song Contest?
4 What was the title of Lena Martell's 1979 number 1 hit?
5 Which television show first broadcast in 1963 became known as *TW3*?

Round 6
1 In which well-known film do a group of children mistake an escaped convict for Jesus?
2 Which English bowler took seven West Indies wickets in the second innings of his test match debut in June 1995?
3 Which member of the English peerage is known for his advocacy of prison reform?
4 Which well-known fictional doctor was created by Max Brand and played in a series of films by Lew Ayres before moving to television in the 1960s?
5 Which US actor appeared in all the following films: *Jesse James*, *The Sun Also Rises*, and *The Black Swan*?

Game 3 — Rounds 4–6

Round 4
1. Norman SCHWARZKOPF
2. Donald SUTHERLAND
3. Santo DOMINGO
4. James LIND
5. Cheryl BAKER

    Quizlink = Surnames of famous OPERA SINGERS
      (Elizabeth Schwarzkopf; Joan Sutherland;
      Placido Domingo; Jenny Lind; Janet Baker)

Round 5
1. *The MILLENNIUM Falcon*
2. *Every SECOND Counts*
3. *'What's Another YEAR?'*
4. *'One DAY at a time'*
5. *That Was The WEEK That Was*

    Quizlink = Periods of TIME

Round 6
1. *Whistle DOWN the Wind*
2. Dominic CORK
3. Lord LONGFORD
4. Doctor KILDARE
5. TYRONE Power

    Quizlink = Names of
    IRISH COUNTIES

Game 4 — Rounds 1-3

Round 1
1. In the original television adaptation of the book *Rich Man, Poor Man*, Nick Nolte played the part of the poor man. Who played the rich man?
2. What was the name of the character in *Are You Being Served?* played by Wendy Richards?
3. In which television comedy series did Liza Goddard play the part of a piano teacher?
4. Who played Daisy Duke in *The Dukes of Hazzard*?
5. Who wrote the world famous book *The Compleat Angler*?

Round 2
1. Which two countries united in 1964 to form the country of Tanzania?
2. Which children's TV cartoon show was about a janitor with a double life as an accident-prone, kung-fu practising, super detective?
3. In which city could you sunbathe on Copacabana beach?
4. Which British colony was founded by Sir Stamford Raffles?
5. What was the title of Sir Thomas More's book about a perfect society?

Round 3
1. Which television quiz game hosted by Michael Barrymore involves the use of a number of televisions?
2. Where, according to the Beatles, did somebody keep his fire engine clean with a clean machine?
3. Which actress played Rebecca in the US comedy show *Cheers*?
4. Which small metallic fastener was invented by the US inventor Walter Hunt?
5. Which accessory carried by a motorist could you also have around your midriff?

Game 4 — Rounds 1–3

Round 1
1. Peter STRAUSS
2. Miss BRAHMS
3. *Roll Over BEETHOVEN*
4. Catherine BACH
5. Isaak WALTON

                       Quizlink = Surnames of
                             COMPOSERS

Round 2
1. Tanganyika and ZANZIBAR
2. *HONG KONG Phooey*
3. RIO de Janeiro
4. SINGAPORE
5. *UTOPIA*

                 Quizlink = Destinations in the series of ROAD
            FILMS starring Bob Hope and Bing Crosby

Round 3
1. *STRIKE it Lucky*
2. Penny LANE
3. Kirsty ALLEY
4. Safety PIN
5. SPARE tyre

                         Quizlink = Terms used in
                            TEN PIN BOWLING

Game 4 — Rounds 4–6

Round 4
1 In which well-known film does the character played by Paul Newman eat 50 eggs?
2 Which female group had a 1981 hit with the song 'Slow Hand'?
3 What name is given to an annual statement of accounts produced by a business?
4 What is the name of the Chinese snack consisting of a pancake filled with vegetables, rolled up, and then fried?
5 Which Alfred Hitchcock film starred Ray Milland and Grace Kelly?

Round 5
1 What was the full name of the musician who was nicknamed 'Jellyroll'?
2 By what name did the ancient Romans know Britain?
3 In which film did Alec Guinness play eight roles?
4 Who was the mistress of Horatio Nelson?
5 Which gangster was portrayed on film by Warren Beatty in 1967?

Round 6
1 To which organization have David Nixon, Tommy Cooper, and Paul Daniels all belonged?
2 *As Seen On TV* starred whom?
3 What do the initials DC stand for in Washington DC?
4 One of the most important events in crown green bowling is named after the Blackpool hotel where it is staged. What is it called?
5 Which anniversary did Queen Victoria celebrate in 1897?

Game 4 — Rounds 4–6

Round 4
1. *Cool HAND Luke*
2. The POINTER Sisters
3. BALANCE sheet
4. SPRING roll
5. *DIAL M For Murder*

> Quizlink = Parts of a
> WATCH or CLOCK

Round 5
1. Ferdinand 'Jellyroll' MORTON
2. ALBION
3. *Kind HEARTS and Coronets*
4. Emma HAMILTON
5. CLYDE Barrow

> Quizlink = Names of Scottish
> FOOTBALL TEAMS

Round 6
1. The Magic CIRCLE
2. VICTORIA Wood
3. DISTRICT of Columbia
4. WATERLOO Cup
5. Diamond JUBILEE

> Quizlink = Names of lines on the
> London UNDERGROUND

Game 5 — Rounds 1–3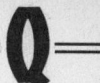

Round 1
1. In which musical work does the character Lieutenant Pinkerton appear?
2. Aboard which vessel did Sir Francis Chichester complete a circumnavigation of the globe in 1967?
3. Which is the world's smallest species of bird?
4. What was the name of the group of gangsters who drove one of the cars in the television cartoon show *Wacky Races*?
5. In which film of 1987 did Harrison Ford play an inventor?

Round 2
1. What name is given to the hydrated form of calcium sulphate that sets hard when it is mixed with water?
2. Which Dutch football team were European champions in three consecutive years of the early 1970s?
3. What is the name of the strong fibrous cord that connects the calf muscle to the heel?
4. Who was the female star of the television show *The Duchess of Malfi*?
5. Who composed the *Symphonie Fantastique*?

Round 3
1. In which novel does the gang leader Colleoni appear?
2. What is the nickname of Coventry City football club?
3. Which singer had a number 1 hit in 1976 with 'Don't Give Up On Us'?
4. In which Charles Dickens novel does Inspector Bucket appear?
5. Which film is generally accepted to be the first 'talkie'?

Game 5 — Rounds 1–3

Round 1
1. *Madame BUTTERFLY*
2. Gipsy MOTH IV
3. BEE humming bird
4. The ANT Hill Mob
5. *MOSQUITO Coast*

                     Quizlink = INSECTS

Round 2
1. Plaster of PARIS
2. AJAX of Amsterdam
3. ACHILLES tendon
4. HELEN Mirren
5. HECTOR Berlioz

         Quizlink = Participants in the
             TROJAN WAR or SIEGE OF TROY

Round 3
1. *Brighton ROCK* by Graham Greene
2. 'The Sky BLUES'
3. David SOUL
4. *Bleak HOUSE*
5. *The JAZZ Singer*

                 Quizlink = Types of MUSIC

Game 5 — Rounds 4–6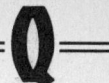

Round 4
1. What is the name of the world's largest monolith?
2. What was the name of the television show in which Tom Baker read and reviewed books for children?
3. What is the common name for the astronomical phenomenon commonly known as the *aurora borealis*?
4. Which group first entered the charts with a song called 'I Get Around'?
5. What was the full name of Alan B'stard's personal assistant in the television comedy show *The New Statesman*?

Round 5
1. In which 1957 film did Frank Sinatra play the part of a night-club entertainer working in San Francisco?
2. What is undoubtedly the most famous novel written by Muriel Spark?
3. Which phrase, originating from the name of a Cambridge horse dealer, means in essence that you get what you are given?
4. Who played the part of the Joker in the *Batman* television series of the 1960s?
5. Which cartoon director created the character of Droopy?

Round 6
1. Who did British boxer Nigel Benn defeat in one round in the first defence of his world middleweight title?
2. What was the title of the only number 1 hit for the group T'Pau?
3. Which British show jumper rode a horse called Mandingo?
4. What was the pen name of writer Jacques Thibault?
5. Who in 1953 founded the organization known as the Samaritans?

Game 5 — Rounds 4–6

Round 4
1. Ayers ROCK (in Australia)
2. *The Book TOWER*
3. The Northern LIGHTS
4. The BEACH Boys
5. PIERS Fletcher-Dervish

> Quizlink = Things associated with the seaside resort of BLACKPOOL

Round 5
1. *PAL Joey*
2. *The PRIME of Miss Jean Brodie*
3. Hobson's CHOICE
4. CESAR Romero
5. TEX Avery

> Quizlink = Brands of DOG FOOD

Round 6
1. IRAN Barkley
2. 'CHINA in Your Hand'
3. Jean GERMANY
4. Anatole FRANCE
5. CHAD Varah

> Quizlink = Names of COUNTRIES

Game 6 — Rounds 1–3

Round 1
1. What was the name of the Scottish heroine remembered for her part in the escape of Bonnie Prince Charlie in 1746?
2. Who was the first person ever to appear on a postage stamp?
3. What was the stage name of the British music hall entertainer Matilda Alice Powles who specialized in male impersonation?
4. What is the name of the damaged sculpture of Aphrodite discovered on the island of Melos in 1820?
5. What was the title of the controversial book about a member of the British royal family published by Andrew Morton in June 1992?

Round 2
1. In which novel by Oliver Goldsmith does the character of Doctor Primrose appear?
2. Which group had a Top 10 hit in 1988 with a song called 'Real Gone Kid'?
3. Whose record of most goals in an English season has stood for over 60 years?
4. Which British rock band was involved in a US court case over subliminal lyrics in the late 1980s?
5. Which British poet and satirist wrote the well-known phrase 'Fools rush in where angels fear to tread'?

Round 3
1. Which song did Frank Ifield take to number 22 in the 1963 charts?
2. In which film was Richard Harris captured by Indians?
3. Which method of mail transportation was operated in the USA in 1860/1?
4. Who is credited with the invention of the revolver?
5. Which television show featured Globelink News?

Game 6 — Rounds 1–3

Round 1
1. FLORA Macdonald
2. Queen VICTORIA
3. VESTA Tilley
4. *VENUS de Milo*
5. *DIANA: Her True Story*

        Quizlink = Names of Roman
                GODDESSES

Round 2
1. *The VICAR of Wakefield*
2. DEACON Blue
3. Dixie DEAN
4. Judas PRIEST
5. Alexander POPE

        Quizlink = Various offices of
          CLERGY or RELIGION

Round 3
1. 'MULE Train'
2. *A Man Called HORSE*
3. The PONY Express
4. Samuel COLT
5. *Drop The Dead DONKEY*

        Quizlink = Names of
          EQUINE creatures

Game 6 — Rounds 4–6

Round 4
1 By what name is the singer Stanley Burrell better known?
2 Which was the first of the Harry Palmer film trilogy?
3 What is the name of the cocktail consisting of vodka and orange juice?
4 Which one word can be all of the following: a small West African monkey; a type of heavy cotton cloth; and a marine mollusc closely related to the whelk?
5 Who was the partner of Chaka Demus on hit songs of the 1990s?

Round 5
1 In which card game are all the cards under seven not used?
2 What was the name of the man known as the Old Pretender?
3 What was the name of the soothsayer in Frankie Howerd's television comedy show *Up Pompeii*?
4 In which film did Sean Connery play a Russian submarine captain?
5 Who was the British lead singer with the pop group the Monkees?

Round 6
1 What is the more common name given to the Chilean pine tree?
2 Which former member of the duo Soft Cell recorded a hit record with Gene Pitney?
3 Which is the only South American country whose official national language is Portuguese?
4 What name is given to a male swan?
5 Which female singer recorded 'Eighth Day' and 'Will You'?

Round 4
1. HAMMER (formerly M C Hammer)
2. *The Ipcress FILE*
3. SCREWDRIVER
4. DRILL
5. PLIERS

        Quizlink = Kinds of TOOLS

Round 5
1. PIQUET
2. James STEWART
3. SENNA
4. *The HUNT For Red October*
5. Davy JONES

        Quizlink = Surnames of WORLD MOTOR RACING CHAMPIONS (Nelson Piquet; Jackie Stewart; Ayrton Senna; James Hunt; Alan Jones)

Round 6
1. MONKEY puzzle
2. Marc ALMOND
3. BRAZIL
4. COB
5. HAZEL O'Connor

        Quizlink = Types of NUT

Game 7 — Rounds 1–3

Round 1
1. British actor Anthony Hopkins won an Oscar in 1991 for his portrayal of which character?
2. What alternative name is given to the Sepoy rebellion of 1857/8?
3. In which film is the central character called Charlie Allnut?
4. What was the title of the 1982 number 1 hit for Paul McCartney and Stevie Wonder?
5. Which *Emmerdale Farm* character died after he accidentally shot himself with his own shotgun?

Round 2
1. In which television show did David Hasselhof drive a car called KITT?
2. Which building replaced St James's Palace in 1837?
3. Who is well known for saying 'Hello, good evening and welcome'?
4. What was the name of singing cowboy Gene Autrey's horse?
5. Who on television shared a prison cell with Lennie Godber?

Round 3
1. Which queen of England reigned for only nine days?
2. Who played the title role in the television series *Sharpe*?
3. In which country were the first ever Commonwealth Games held?
4. Which actor plays the robot in *Star Trek The Next Generation*?
5. In which Ealing comedy film of 1957 did Alec Guinness play the part of a seasick sailor who takes charge of a Victorian pier?

Game 7 — Rounds 1–3

Round 1
1. HANNIBAL Lecter
2. The INDIAN Mutiny
3. *The AFRICAN Queen*
4. 'Ebony and IVORY'
5. Jackie MERRICK

Quizlink = All words connected with the ELEPHANT
(Hannibal was the Carthaginian general who reputedly led a herd of elephants across the Alps; John Merrick was the name of the man who became known as the Elephant Man)

Round 2
1. *KNIGHT Rider*
2. BUCKINGHAM Palace
3. David FROST
4. CHAMPION
5. Norman Stanley FLETCHER (in *Porridge*)

Quizlink = Names of GRAND NATIONAL-winning JOCKEYS
(Steve Knight rode Maori Venture in 1987; John Buckingham rode Foinavon in 1967; Jimmy Frost rode Little Polveir in 1989; Bob Champion rode Aldaniti in 1981; and Brian Fletcher rode Red Rum to two of his three victories and also partnered Red Alligator in 1968)

Round 3
1. Lady Jane GREY
2. Sean BEAN
3. CANADA
4. BRENT Spiner
5. *BARNACLE Bill*

Quizlink = Types of GEESE

Game 7 — Rounds 4–6

Round 4
1 Where did Tolkien set his *Lord of the Rings* trilogy?
2 In which 1971 film did Dustin Hoffman play a character living in Cornwall?
3 Almost 500 British soldiers died in one action on 25 Oct 1854. How is this incident known today?
4 Who served as general secretary of the TUC from 1970–74?
5 What was the title of the second number 1 hit for the Hollies?

Round 5
1 What is the SI unit of illumination?
2 Jan and Dean had a 1963 hit in the British charts with a song whose title was concerned with a particular water sport. What was the title of the song?
3 Who was the flighty spirit in the Shakespeare play *The Tempest*?
4 What name is given to the electric decorations used on Christmas trees?
5 In the printing trade, which word is used to describe text which is thicker than usual in order to give it prominence?

Round 6
1 Who was the female star of the film *The Woman in Red*?
2 Which politician during the 1960s and 1970s served at various times as chancellor of the Exchequer, home secretary, foreign secretary, and prime minister?
3 What is the better-known title of the man who is also Duke of Cornwall?
4 Which television show of the 1980s was written by, directed by, and also starred the actor Michael Landon?
5 What name is given to an arrangement of ropes and pulleys used for hoisting or hauling?

Game 7 — Rounds 4–6

Round 4
1. MIDDLE Earth
2. *STRAW Dogs*
3. The Charge of the LIGHT Brigade
4. Vic FEATHER
5. 'He Ain't HEAVY He's My Brother'

                Quizlink = BOXING WEIGHTS

Round 5
1. The LUX
2. 'SURF City'
3. ARIEL
4. FAIRY lights
5. BOLD

                Quizlink = Brand names of
                WASHING POWDERS

Round 6
1. KELLY Le Brock
2. James CALLAGHAN
3. The Prince of WALES
4. *HIGHWAY To Heaven*
5. BLOCK and tackle

Quizlink = Characters played in films by CLINT EASTWOOD
(Kelly in *Kelly's Heroes*; Callaghan in the *Dirty Harry* series;
Wales in *The Outlaw Josey Wales*; Highway in *Heartbreak
Ridge*; and Block in *Tightrope*)

Game 8 — Rounds 1–3

Round 1
1. Who was the first wife of England's King Henry VIII?
2. What was the name of the character played by Rodney Bewes in the television comedy show *The Likely Lads*?
3. Which novel is set in the magic land of St Brandan's Isle?
4. In which film do John Wayne and Kirk Douglas plan to ambush a mining contractor's gold shipment?
5. Which football team lost their league status in 1972?

Round 2
1. With which historical event was *The Iliad* concerned?
2. What was the well-known invention of Frank Whittle?
3. Which character did Ronald Allen play in the now defunct television soap, *Crossroads*?
4. Which ship was sunk after an explosion in Auckland harbour, New Zealand, in July 1985?
5. What is the better-known name of the plant belladonna?

Round 3
1. Who said that the report of his death was an exaggeration?
2. What did Shylock want to satisfy the debt owed to him in Shakespeare's play, *The Merchant of Venice*?
3. What name is given to the punctuation mark that consists of two dots, one above the other?
4. Who was the Italian film director best known for his work on the so-called spaghetti westerns?
5. Which British woman won an Olympic long jump gold medal in 1964?

Game 8 — Rounds 1–3

Round 1
1. CATHERINE of Aragon
2. Bob FERRIS
3. *The WATER Babies* by Charles Kingsley
4. *The War WAGON*
5. BARROW

Quizlink = Types of WHEEL

Round 2
1. The TROJAN War
2. The JET engine
3. David HUNTER
4. The Greenpeace ship *Rainbow WARRIOR*
5. Deadly NIGHTSHADE

Quizlink = Names of television's GLADIATORS

Round 3
1. MARK Twain
2. A POUND of flesh
3. COLON
4. Sergio LEONE
5. Mary RAND

Quizlink = World CURRENCIES (Mark – Germany; Pound – UK; Colon – El Salvador; Leone – Sierra Leone; Rand – South Africa)

Game 8 — Rounds 4–6

Round 4

1 What name is given to the Chinese method of cooking where small pieces of food are mixed together and cooked rapidly in hot oil?
2 On television, what is the name of Aidensfield's police constable?
3 What is the name of the traditional Scottish breakfast dish of boiled oatmeal?
4 What was the title of the first British hit song for Suzi Quatro?
5 What is a ewer?

Round 5

1 Chuck Connors played the title role in the television western show *The Rifleman*. What was the name of his character?
2 Who composed *A German Requiem* in 1868?
3 Who became famous for using a rowing boat to rescue some of the crew of the *SS Forfarshire*?
4 Who created the slobbish cultural attaché Les Patterson?
5 Who is remembered for his transposition of the initial letters of words, resulting in such phrases as 'A scoop of boy trouts'?

Round 6

1 Which actor played one of *The Magnificent Seven* and also appeared in the film *Von Ryan's Express*?
2 Which device for lifting water was invented by, and named after, an ancient Greek mathematician?
3 Who has played television characters called Oz and Spender?
4 Which single word is used to describe equipment used in horse riding?
5 Which indoor game is governed in the USA by the ABC?

Game 8 — Rounds 4–6

Round 4
1. STIR frying
2. NICK Rowan (played by Nick Berry in *Heartbeat*)
3. PORRIDGE
4. 'CAN the Can'
5. A large water JUG

Quizlink = Slang terms for
PRISON or JAIL

Round 5
1. LUCAS McCain
2. Johannes BRAHMS
3. GRACE Darling
4. Barry HUMPHRIES
5. William SPOONER

Quizlink = Surnames of characters from the television comedy show *ARE YOU BEING SERVED?*

Round 6
1. BRAD Dexter
2. Archimedes SCREW
3. Jimmy NAIL
4. TACK
5. Ten PIN bowling

Quizlink = Types of
FASTENER

Game 9 — Rounds 1–3

Round 1
1 What is the name of the 822 ft high hill situated close to Holyrood House and overlooking the city of Edinburgh?
2 Who composed the overture *Fingal's Cave*?
3 What is the last letter of the Greek alphabet?
4 What name is given to the long spikes of flowers found hanging on trees such as the hazel or willow?
5 According to the Old Testament, which royal female visited King Solomon?

Round 2
1 Who was the Roman equivalent of Eros?
2 Who replaced Barbara Bel Geddes in the TV show *Dallas*?
3 What is visible to people on Earth once every 76 years?
4 Which US all-girl group had their first British chart success in 1987 with a song called 'Edge of a Broken Heart'?
5 As what did Anna Pavlova become famous?

Round 3
1 Which group had a hit with the song 'To Know Him Is To Love Him'?
2 What was the title of the first in the series of *Indiana Jones* films?
3 Which group had a hit with the song 'Lyin' Eyes'?
4 Which people invaded England in the year AD 792?
5 What were the names of the rival gangs in the musical film *West Side Story*?

Game 9 — Rounds 1–3

Round 1
1. ARTHUR'S seat
2. FELIX Mendelssohn
3. OMEGA
4. CATKINS
5. The queen of SHEBA

Quizlink = Brands of
CAT FOOD

Round 2
1. CUPID
2. DONNA Reed
3. Halley's COMET
4. VIXEN
5. Ballet DANCER

Quizlink = Names of REINDEER
employed by Santa Claus

Round 3
1. The Teddy BEARS
2. *RAIDERS Of The Lost Ark*
3. The EAGLES
4. The VIKINGS
5. The JETS and the Sharks

Quizlink = Nicknames of AMERICAN FOOTBALL TEAMS
(Chicago Bears; Los Angeles Raiders; Philadelphia Eagles;
Minnesota Vikings; New York Jets)

Game 9 — Rounds 4–6

Round 4

1. Who said 'This is not the end, it is not even the beginning of the end.'?
2. Who was the lead singer with the 1980s pop group Altered Images?
3. What is the name of the authority that controls lighthouses and buoys around the coast of England and Wales?
4. What are the names of the two different breeds of corgi dog?
5. Which television comedy character played by Bill Maynard frequently said 'Magic our Maurice'?

Round 5

1. The biblical brothers James and John were known as the Sons of Thunder. Who was their father?
2. Which well-known author wrote *Under Milk Wood*?
3. Who carried a pet owl around in her pocket during the Crimean War?
4. In which irreverent comedy film was the title role played by Graham Chapman?
5. Which former television news reader went on to present a Channel 4 programme for senior citizens?

Round 6

1. Which famous Englishman said shortly before his death, 'I thank God that I have done my duty.'?
2. Who played the part of Huggy Bear in the television show *Starsky And Hutch*?
3. Which explorer was killed by natives in the Philippines in 1521?
4. In which television show is there a character called Eddie Hitler?
5. Who was the 1960 Olympic light heavyweight boxing champion?

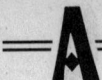

Game 9 — Rounds 4–6

Round 4
1. Sir Winston CHURCHILL
2. CLARE Grogan
3. TRINITY House
4. Cardigan and PEMBROKE
5. SELWYN Froggitt

> Quizlink = Names of COLLEGES at CAMBRIDGE UNIVERSITY

Round 5
1. ZEBEDEE
2. DYLAN Thomas
3. FLORENCE Nightingale
4. *The Life Of BRIAN*
5. Robert DOUGAL

> Quizlink = Characters from the children's television puppet show *THE MAGIC ROUNDABOUT*

Round 6
1. HORATIO Nelson
2. ANTONIO Fargas
3. FERDINAND Magellan
4. *BOTTOM*
5. CASSIUS Clay

> Quizlink = SHAKESPEAREAN CHARACTERS
> (Horatio – *Hamlet*; Antonio – *The Merchant Of Venice*; Ferdinand – *The Tempest*; Bottom – *A Midsummer Night's Dream*; Cassius – *Julius Caesar*)

Game 10 — Rounds 1–3

Round 1
1. Which actress plays the character Dorian Green on television?
2. Which station do you pass first at the start of a game of Monopoly?
3. Which US woman was killed in a notorious car crash at Chappaquiddick in 1969?
4. What does the road sign showing a cow inside a red circle signify?
5. Who starred opposite Bruce Willis in the television show *Moonlighting*?

Round 2
1. Which writer's only novel was *Gone With The Wind*?
2. Who played the detective Frank Cannon on television?
3. Who had companions called Wilson, Bowers, Evans, and Oates?
4. Who wrote the novel *Rich Man, Poor Man*?
5. What was the middle name of the famous general who died with his troops at the Battle of Little Big Horn in 1876?

Round 3
1. Who played the part of the wife in the television show *Macmillan And Wife*?
2. Where could you see the burial place known as Poets' Corner?
3. In which historical film of 1968 did Katharine Hepburn and Peter O'Toole play a married couple?
4. Who rode 100/1 outsider Foinavon to victory in the 1967 Grand National?
5. What is the traditional gift for a 15th wedding anniversary?

Game 10 — Rounds 1–3

Round 1
1. Leslie JOSEPH
2. KINGS Cross Station
3. MARY Jo Kopechne
4. CATTLE crossing
5. Cybil SHEPHERD

> Quizlink = All present in the manger
> where JESUS was born

Round 2
1. Margaret MITCHELL
2. William CONRAD
3. Robert Falcon SCOTT
4. IRWIN Shaw
5. ARMSTRONG (George Armstrong Custer)

> Quizlink = ASTRONAUTS who have
> walked on the MOON

Round 3
1. Susan ST JAMES
2. WESTMINSTER Abbey
3. *The Lion In WINTER*
4. John BUCKINGHAM
5. CRYSTAL

> Quizlink = Names of well-known
> PALACES

Game 10 — Rounds 4–6

Round 4

1. Which horse won the King George VI Chase three times in the 1980s?
2. What is the name of the snooty character played by Patricia Routledge in the television comedy show *Keeping Up Appearances*?
3. What name is given to the system of connecting computer devices in a series, so that the first device is connected to the second, the second to the third, and so on?
4. Which Canadian group had a hit with a song called 'Which Way You Going Billy' in 1970?
5. Which female character in literature often threatened to 'scream and scream and scream'?

Round 5

1. Which British heavyweight boxer was knocked out in world title fights by both Floyd Paterson and Muhammad Ali?
2. Which former member of the Eagles released a solo album entitled *Building The Perfect Beast*?
3. What was the name of the television character played by Ralph Waite in a series set in the US depression?
4. What is the capital city of Jamaica?
5. What was the real name of actor John Carradine who died in 1988?

Round 6

1. Which fictional character made his first appearance in the 1929 story *The Roman Hat Mystery*?
2. Which film of 1973 starring Robert Redford and Paul Newman won the Oscar for best picture?
3. In which 1989 film did Rick Moranis play an inventor who had trouble with his children?
4. What was the title of the early television comedy show in which Charlie Drake played an unemployable layabout?
5. Which word describes a pilotless, radio controlled aircraft?

Game 10 — Rounds 4–6

Round 4
1 Desert ORCHID
2 HYACINTH Bucket
3 DAISY chaining
4 The POPPY Family
5 VIOLET Elizabeth Bott

                Quizlink = FLOWERS

Round 5
1 Brian LONDON
2 Don HENLEY
3 John WALTON
4 KINGSTON
5 RICHMOND Reed

                Quizlink = Places situated on the
                           RIVER THAMES

Round 6
1 Ellery QUEEN
2 *The STING*
3 *HONEY, I Shrunk The Kids*
4 *The WORKER*
5 DRONE

                Quizlink = Words connected with BEES

Game 11 — Rounds 1–3

Round 1
1. Which well-known explorer set sail aboard the *Santa Maria* in the year 1492?
2. Who was the target of the assassin in the film *Day of the Jackal*?
3. Who became the first leader of an independent Kenya in 1964?
4. Who was assassinated on 22 Nov 1963?
5. Which Italian artist painted the world famous *Mona Lisa*?

Round 2
1. Which Compton Mackenzie novel centres on a 1943 shipwreck?
2. What is the capital city of Trinidad and Tobago?
3. In which variation of a well-known card game does each player receive ten cards?
4. In the book *Treasure Island* which line follows 'Fifteen men on the dead man's chest.'?
5. Which girl's name gave the Four Seasons a hit in 1962?

Round 3
1. Which singer's only British number 1 hit was 'Runaway'?
2. Who plays the part of Lacey in the television show *Cagney and Lacey*?
3. Which device protecting the city of London was operated for the first time in 1984?
4. Who played Uncle Mort in the television comedy show *I Didn't Know You Cared*?
5. Who played the part of Princess Leia in the first of the *Star Wars* series of films?

Game 11 — Rounds 1–3

Round 1
1. CHRISTOPHER COLUMBUS
2. CHARLES DE GAULLE
3. JOMO KENYATTA
4. JOHN F KENNEDY
5. LEONARDO DA VINCI

Quizlink = All names of INTERNATIONAL AIRPORTS
(Christopher Columbus serves Genoa; Charles de Gaulle serves Paris; Jomo Kenyatta serves Nairobi; John F Kennedy serves New York; and Leonardo da Vinci serves Rome)

Round 2
1. *WHISKY Galore*
2. PORT of Spain
3. GIN rummy
4. 'Yo ho ho and a bottle of RUM!'
5. SHERRY

Quizlink = ALCOHOLIC DRINKS

Round 3
1. Del SHANNON
2. TYNE Daly
3. The THAMES flood barrier
4. Robin BAILEY
5. Carrie FISHER

Quizlink = Names of SHIPPING FORECAST AREAS

Game 11 — Rounds 4–6

Round 4
1 Which famous woman committed suicide after the Battle of Actium in 31 BC?
2 What is the old name for the chemical element now called sulphur?
3 Which Greek god was the son of Zeus and brother of Artemis?
4 For which man was Hampton Court built?
5 Which character in the television comedy series *Are You Being Served?* was played by Frank Thornton?

Round 5
1 What 'burst' in 1720, causing the financial ruin of thousands of investors?
2 In which stretch of water is the island of Lundy situated?
3 In which Spanish city can you see the Alhambra, a Moorish citadel and palace?
4 Who was the Australian cricket captain on the 1993 tour of England?
5 Which word describes any one of the imaginary lines connecting the North and South Poles and running at right angles to the equator?

Round 6
1 Which US tennis player did Bjorn Borg beat to win his fourth consecutive Wimbledon singles title?
2 Which creature gives its name to a protein found in human blood?
3 Who has always been the presenter of the teenage quiz show *Blockbusters*?
4 Which Latin term means 'an equal exchange or substitution'?
5 Which equine creature is particularly associated with the Shetland Islands?

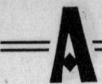

Game 11 — Rounds 4–6

Round 4
1. CLEOPATRA
2. BRIMSTONE
3. APOLLO
4. CARDINAL Wolsey
5. Captain PEACOCK

Quizlink = Species of BUTTERFLY

Round 5
1. The SOUTH sea bubble
2. The Bristol CHANNEL
3. GRANADA
4. Allan BORDER
5. MERIDIAN

Quizlink = Names of independent TELEVISION COMPANIES

Round 6
1. Roscoe TANNER
2. The Rhesus MONKEY
3. BOB Holness
4. QUID pro quo
5. Shetland PONY

Quizlink = Slang terms for particular amounts of MONEY
(Tanner = 6 old pence; Monkey = £500; Bob = 1 old shilling or 12 old pence; Quid = £1; and Pony = £25)

Game 12 — Rounds 1–3

Round 1
1 Who kidnapped Helen of Troy and precipitated the Trojan War?
2 By what title was Arthur Wellesley better known?
3 Which song was the highest placed chart entry for Ultravox?
4 In the USA in 1949, Mrs I Toguri d'Aquino was sentenced to ten years in prison for treason. By what name was she known during World War II?
5 Which character did Peter Lorre play in the film *The Maltese Falcon*?

Round 2
1 On which date does St George's day fall?
2 Who wrote *Adolf Hitler, My Part In His Downfall*?
3 What was the name of the nurse lusted after by Arkwright in the television comedy show *Open All Hours*?
4 What was the title of the first British hit for Buddy Holly?
5 Which British soldier of the 18th century spent most of his life in India?

Round 3
1 Which television quiz show presented by Bob Monkhouse was based on the game of bingo?
2 In which film did Clint Eastwood play an Arizona sheriff charged with taking an escaped killer back to New York?
3 What was the title of the sequel to the television show *Porridge*?
4 What was the name of the pet dog owned by Elizabeth Barrett Browning?
5 How were Lenny Henry, Tracy Ullman, and David Copperfield known collectively in a television comedy show?

Game 12 — Rounds 1–3

Round 1
1. PARIS
2. The Duke of WELLINGTON
3. 'VIENNA'
4. TOKYO Rose
5. Joel CAIRO

Quizlink = CAPITAL CITIES

Round 2
1. 23 APRIL
2. SPIKE Milligan
3. GLADYS Emmanuel
4. 'PEGGY Sue'
5. Robert CLIVE

Quizlink = Names of characters from the television show *HI-DE-HI*

Round 3
1. *Bob's FULL HOUSE*
2. *Coogan's BLUFF*
3. *Going STRAIGHT*
4. FLUSH
5. *THREE OF A KIND*

Quizlink = Terms used in the game of POKER

Game 12 — Rounds 4–6

Round 4
1 Which Australian painter is well known for his portraits of the outlaw Ned Kelly?
2 On which day of the year is the Eton wall game traditionally played?
3 In which television show did Max Baer and Donna Douglas play brother and sister?
4 What name was given to the flight of Chinese communists led by Mao Tse Tung in 1934?
5 When Armstrong and Aldrin walked on the Moon for the first time in 1969, who remained in the command module?

Round 5
1 What in mythology was suspended by a single horse hair?
2 Which 1924 play by Sean O'Casey tells of life in a Dublin slum?
3 Which is the largest city in the state of Nebraska?
4 What was the title of Freda Payne's number 1 hit?
5 In which state of the USA is Salt Lake City?

Round 6
1 Born in 1820, she became famous for her pioneering medical work during the Crimean War. Who was she?
2 Born in 1812, at the age of 12 he was put to work in Warren's boot blacking factory. He became one of England's most celebrated novelists. Who was he?
3 Born in 1642, he devised the three laws of motion and is credited with the discovery of gravity. Who was he?
4 Born in 1781, he built the famous *Rocket* steam locomotive. Who was he?
5 Born in 1632, he designed 51 churches, the most famous being St Paul's Cathedral in London. Who was he?

Game 12 — Rounds 4–6

Round 4
1 Sydney NOLAN
2 St ANDREW'S Day
3 *The BEVERLY Hillbillies*
4 The long MARCH
5 Michael COLLINS

Quizlink = Surnames of well-known SISTERS (the Nolan, Andrews, and Beverly sisters are all singing groups; the March sisters featured in the book *Little Women*; and the Collins sisters are Jackie, the writer, and Joan, the actress)

Round 5
1 The SWORD of Damocles
2 *JUNO and the Paycock*
3 OMAHA
4 'Band of GOLD'
5 UTAH

Quizlink = CODE NAMES given to the BEACHES used in the D Day landings of World War II

Round 6
1 FLORENCE NIGHTINGALE
2 CHARLES DICKENS
3 ISAAC NEWTON
4 GEORGE STEPHENSON
5 CHRISTOPHER WREN

Quizlink = All people whose portraits appear or have appeared in the past on British BANK NOTES

Game 13 — Rounds 1–3

Round 1
1 Which *Coronation Street* character was widowed when her husband was killed by armed raiders at his place of work?
2 Who wrote the series of *Lassie* books?
3 Which pair of private detectives were played on television by Derek Martin and Nigel Planer?
4 Which group made the 1976 album *A Day at the Races*?
5 Who won the first of 20 Wimbledon titles in 1966?

Round 2
1 Which Brazilian motor racing driver was Formula One world champion in 1981, 1983, and 1987?
2 Which film of 1977 is concerned with the disastrous allied landings at Arnhem during World War II?
3 Which US rap duo reached number 1 in the British charts in 1990 with a song called 'The Power'?
4 What is the common name of the flower *Kniphofia*?
5 Where are the headquarters of British horse racing?

Round 3
1 Which song was a number 1 hit for Enya in 1988?
2 Who was the successful British commander at the Battle of Waterloo?
3 After Jersey and Guernsey, which is the next largest of the Channel Islands?
4 Of which country is Sofia the capital city?
5 Which US national park covers part of the states of Wyoming, Idaho, and Montana and contains the famous geyser known as Old Faithful?

Game 13 — Rounds 1–3

Round 1
1. Emily BISHOP
2. Eric KNIGHT
3. *KING and CASTLE*
4. QUEEN
5. Billie Jean KING

        Quizlink = CHESS pieces

Round 2
1. Nelson PIQUET
2. *A BRIDGE Too Far*
3. SNAP
4. Red hot POKER
5. NEWMARKET

        Quizlink = CARD GAMES

Round 3
1. 'ORINOCO Flow'
2. The Duke of WELLINGTON
3. ALDERNEY
4. BULGARIA
5. YELLOWSTONE National Park

        Quizlink = Names of WOMBLES from the children's television show *The Wombles*

Game 13 — Rounds 4–6

Round 4

1 What was the surname of Richard and Karen, the singing duo who had several hits in the British charts during the 1970s?
2 Who lost his British heavyweight boxing title to Joe Bugner in 1971?
3 Who plays the character Betty Turpin in the TV show *Coronation Street*?
4 Who did Kenneth Clarke succeed as home secretary in 1992?
5 Who was the leader of the mutiny against Captain William Bligh aboard *HMS Bounty* in 1789?

Round 5

1 Which football team plays its home matches at the Manor Ground?
2 Which company manufactured the famous Electra Glide motorcycle?
3 Who once married a lady called Teresa Draco?
4 In which film of 1936 did Fred Astaire sing 'Let's face the music and dance'?
5 A famous US actress, she died in 1942. Her last three films were *They Knew What She Wanted*, *Mr and Mrs Smith*, and *To Be Or Not To Be*. Who was she?

Round 6

1 Who is the leader of the Monster Raving Loony Party?
2 Minnie Riperton had a number 2 hit in 1975. With which song?
3 Which well-known artist painted *Flatford Mill*?
4 Which book by Boris Pasternak was made into a film starring Julie Christie?
5 If you are unfortunate enough, you may be given a dose of nitrous oxide at the dentist's. What is the more common name of nitrous oxide?

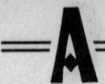

Game 13 — Rounds 4–6

Round 4
1. CARPENTER
2. Henry COOPER
3. Betty DRIVER
4. Kenneth BAKER
5. FLETCHER Christian

Quizlink = OCCUPATIONS

Round 5
1. OXFORD United
2. HARLEY Davidson
3. James BOND
4. *Follow the FLEET*
5. Carole LOMBARD

Quizlink = Famous LONDON STREETS

Round 6
1. SCREAMING Lord Sutch
2. 'LOVING You'
3. John CONSTABLE
4. *DOCTOR Zhivago*
5. LAUGHING gas

Quizlink = Titles of films in the *CARRY ON* series

Game 14 — Rounds 1–3

Round 1
1 Which 1983 film of a Graham Greene novel starred Michael Caine and Richard Gere?
2 What name is shared by mountain ranges in Spain and the USA?
3 Which Spanish word describes a religious festival or celebration especially on a Saint's Day?
4 Which constellation is depicted as the Hunter?
5 In which murder film of 1960 did Noel Trevarthan play an out-of-work actor?

Round 2
1 What is advertised as 'the mint with the hole'?
2 Which West End musical was written by an ex-member of ABBA?
3 Which group had a hit with 'It's Raining'?
4 Its scientific name is *gryllus campestris*; what is it?
5 Which school did Tom Brown attend in the novel by Thomas Hughes?

Round 3
1 In which film did James Cagney proclaim, 'Made it Ma, top of the world.'?
2 Which British regiment is particularly associated with the county of Yorkshire?
3 Which oily blister-inducing liquid has been used as a poison during warfare?
4 Who was referred to in a children's comic as 'our Indian chum'?
5 The first English actress to win the Oscar for best actress did so in 1939. What was the name of the character she portrayed?

Game 14 — Rounds 1–3

Round 1
1 *The Honorary CONSUL*
2 SIERRA Nevada
3 FIESTA
4 ORION
5 *ESCORT For Hire*

        Quizlink = Makes of FORD CARS
                past or present

Round 2
1 POLO
2 *CHESS*
3 DARTS
4 CRICKET (the insect)
5 RUGBY

        Quizlink = GAMES or SPORTS

Round 3
1 WHITE Heat
2 The GREEN Howards
3 MUSTARD gas
4 Little PLUM
5 SCARLETT O'Hara (in *Gone With the Wind*)

        Quizlink = Characters from the
              game of CLUEDO

Game 14 — Rounds 4–6

Round 4

1. Which property on a Monopoly board is immediately to the left of Kings Cross Station?
2. Who created the comic characters Stavros and Loadsamoney?
3. What name is commonly given to the line of longitude lying at 0 degrees?
4. What is the official residence of the Archbishop of Canterbury?
5. What is Cockney rhyming slang for the word 'hair'?

Round 5

1. Which US male/female duo had a British Top 10 hit in 1986 with a song called 'I Can't Wait'?
2. Who played Mariette Larkin on television?
3. Which film starring Charlton Heston is concerned with the aftermath of germ warfare?
4. Which North Sea oil rig exploded in 1988, resulting in the tragic deaths of 167 men?
5. Which word describes the flat area of alluvial deposits at the mouth of some rivers?

Round 6

1. Which group had a number 1 hit with 'Billy Don't be a Hero'?
2. Who is the chairman of Tottenham Hotspur Football Club and founder of the Amstrad company?
3. By what nickname was actress Jean Harlow known?
4. Which country on the coast of West Africa has a capital city called Yamoussoukro?
5. What was the name of the Lone Ranger's horse?

Game 14 — Rounds 4–6

Round 4
1. The Angel ISLINGTON
2. Harry ENFIELD
3. The GREENWICH Meridian
4. LAMBETH Palace
5. BARNET fair

       Quizlink = Names of LONDON BOROUGHS

Round 5
1. NU Shooz
2. Catherine ZETA Jones (in *The Darling Buds of May*)
3. *The OMEGA Man*
4. Piper ALPHA
5. DELTA

       Quizlink = LETTERS of the
       GREEK ALPHABET

Round 6
1. Paper LACE
2. Alan SUGAR
3. The PLATINUM Blonde
4. IVORY Coast
5. SILVER

       Quizlink = Traditional gifts for
       WEDDING ANNIVERSARIES

Game 15 — Rounds 1–3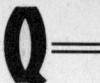

Round 1

1. What name was given to the political uprising that took place in China in 1900?
2. Which television show featured a character called Richard de Vere?
3. What name is given to the drink consisting of a mixture of advocaat and lemonade?
4. Which well-known historical figure first described England as a nation of shopkeepers?
5. Who had a Top 10 hit with a song called 'What is Love?' in 1983?

Round 2

1. What name was given to the sacred gold-covered wooden chest identified by the Hebrews with God?
2. Who became prime minister of Great Britain on the resignation of Lord Salisbury in 1902?
3. Who died when his speedboat *Bluebird* crashed on Coniston Water in 1967?
4. Which song by Paul McCartney spent nine weeks at number 1 in the British charts during the winter of 1977–78?
5. Which US actor appeared in the television series *Maverick* as Bat Masterson, and also appeared in the films *Benji* and *A Man For Hanging*?

Round 3

1. Which character did Linda Thorson play in the television series *The Avengers*?
2. Which Scottish football club is nicknamed 'the Accies'?
3. Who won the Oscar as best supporting actor for his role in the film *Cool Hand Luke*?
4. What was the name of the bus driver played by Reg Varney in the TV comedy show *On The Buses*?
5. Which red-haired Irish actress starred with John Wayne in the film *The Quiet Man*?

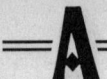

Game 15 — Rounds 1–3

Round 1
1. The BOXER rebellion
2. *To The MANOR Born*
3. SNOWBALL
4. NAPOLEON Bonaparte
5. Howard JONES

   Quizlink = *ANIMAL FARM* by George Orwell (Boxer was a horse; Napoleon and Snowball were pigs; Mr Jones owned the farm; and the farm itself was called Manor Farm)

Round 2
1. The Ark of the COVENANT
2. Arthur James BALFOUR
3. Donald CAMPBELL
4. 'MULL of Kintyre'
5. Peter BRECK

   Quizlink = *KIDNAPPED* by Robert Louis Stevenson (*Covenant* was the name of the ship onto which David Balfour was taken after being kidnapped; Alan Breck was his companion; who, with him, witnessed the murder of Colin Campbell on the island of Mull)

Round 3
1. TARA King
2. HAMILTON Academicals
3. George KENNEDY
4. Stan BUTLER
5. Maureen O'HARA

   Quizlink = *GONE WITH THE WIND* by Margaret Mitchell (Tara was the name of the plantation where Scarlett O'Hara lived; Charles Hamilton, Frank Kennedy, and Rhett Butler were Scarlett's three husbands)

Game 15 — Rounds 4–6

Round 4

1. Which dog, according to legend, watched over his master's grave for 14 years?
2. What type of fruit is a morello?
3. Which British boxer from the city of York was unsuccessful in challenges to both Nigel Benn and Chris Eubank for their world titles?
4. What was the original name of the character played in *Coronation Street* by Eileen Derbyshire?
5. Which famous British sportsman was champion jockey on 26 occasions between 1925 and 1953?

Round 5

1. Which swimmer won seven gold medals at the 1972 Olympic Games in Munich?
2. Who won a Pulitzer Prize for his novel *The Bridge of San Luis Rey*?
3. Which character did Cameron Mitchell play in the TV western series *The High Chaparral*?
4. What was the title of Ralph McTell's 'capital' hit of 1974?
5. In which region of the Yukon was gold discovered in 1896?

Round 6

1. What was the name of the maid played by Connie Booth in the television comedy series *Fawlty Towers*?
2. Who famously became lost during the Paris–Dakar rally of 1982?
3. Which line follows 'Oh, East is East and West is West'?
4. What is the slang term describing a drink containing a drug to render the drinker unconscious?
5. Who created the characters Samuel Whiskers and Mrs Tiggywinkle?

Game 15 — Rounds 4–6

Round 4
1. GREYFRIARS Bobby
2. A CHERRY
3. Henry WHARTON
4. Emily NUGENT
5. Sir Gordon RICHARDS

Quizlink = Any of the 'BILLY BUNTER' stories (Greyfriars was the school attended by Bunter and his schoolmates: Harry Wharton; Bob Cherry; and Frank Nugent; in the stories by Frank Richards)

Round 5
1. Mark SPITZ
2. THORNTON Wilder
3. BUCK Cannon
4. 'Streets of LONDON'
5. The KLONDIKE

Quizlink = *CALL OF THE WILD* by Jack London (Spitz and Buck were dogs; Buck was rescued by prospector John Thornton; and eventually went to live wild in the Klondike; in the book by Jack London)

Round 6
1. POLLY
2. Mark THATCHER
3. 'And never the TWAIN shall meet' in *The Ballad of East and West* by Rudyard Kipling
4. Mickey FINN
5. Beatrix POTTER

Quizlink = *The Adventures of TOM SAWYER* by Mark Twain (Polly was the name of Tom's aunt; Huckleberry Finn was his friend. Together they witnessed a murder of which Muff Potter, the town drunk, was accused. Becky Thatcher was Tom's sweetheart in the book by Mark Twain)

Game 16 — Rounds 1–3

Round 1
1. In which musical film of 1948 do three of the characters sing the song 'Busy Doin' Nothin''?
2. Which song, written by James Connell in 1889, is considered to be the anthem of the Labour movement?
3. Which government department is responsible for the registration of trademarks and industrial designs?
4. What name is given to the type of competition in which all competitors play each other to decide the winner?
5. Which company advertised itself with the slogan '57 varieties'?

Round 2
1. Which female group had a hit in 1981 with 'Slowhand'?
2. Aboard which ship did Charles Darwin travel from 1831–36?
3. What code name was given to the allied invasion of Sicily in 1943?
4. What was the name of the idiot private in the *Bilko* TV show?
5. What was the occupation of Robert de Niro in the film *Raging Bull*?

Round 3
1. Which horse ridden by Hywel Davies won the 1984 Grand National?
2. In which 1982 film did Julie Andrews pose as a female impersonator?
3. Which football club won the FA Cup in 1961/2 and again in 1981/2?
4. In which 1937 film is Cary Grant visited by two friendly ghosts?
5. Which girl's name gave Barry Manilow a hit song in 1975?

Game 16 — Rounds 1–3

Round 1

1. *A Connecticut YANKEE in King Arthur's Court*
2. 'The Red FLAG'
3. The PATENT Office
4. ROUND ROBIN
5. HEINZ

Quizlink = Types of multiple
BETS in HORSE RACING

Round 2

1. The POINTER Sisters
2. *HMS BEAGLE*
3. Operation HUSKY
4. Duane DOBERMAN
5. He was a BOXER

Quizlink = Breeds of DOG

Round 3

1. Hallo DANDY
2. *VICTOR, Victoria*
3. Tottenham HOTSPUR
4. *TOPPER*
5. MANDY

Quizlink = Names of
children's COMICS

Game 16 — Rounds 4–6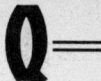

Round 4
1 Of what is pumpernickel a variety?
2 Which character was played by Richard Gibson in the television comedy show *'Allo 'Allo*?
3 What name is given to a female swan?
4 Which actor sang the song 'Get Me to the Church on Time' in the film *My Fair Lady*?
5 Which singer had a number 1 hit with 'Space Oddity'?

Round 5
1 Which music hall entertainer was known as 'the Cheeky Chappie'?
2 Who wrote the poem 'The Charge of the Light Brigade'?
3 Which two rivers converge at New York City?
4 Who had a Top 10 hit with 'In Your Eyes' in 1983?
5 What was the real life name of super hero Spiderman?

Round 6
1 Who wrote *The Mill on the Floss*?
2 Which famous film of 1941 was concerned with a statue of a bird?
3 What name did the American Indians give to early steam locomotives in the wild west?
4 What was the name of John Cannon's wife and Manolito's sister in the television western show *The High Chaparral*?
5 What general term is used to describe the 20 republics of Central and South America where the Romance languages are spoken?

Game 16 — Rounds 4–6

Round 4
1. BREAD
2. Herr FLICK
3. PEN
4. STANLEY Holloway
5. David BOWIE

                Quizlink = Types of KNIVES

Round 5
1. MAX Miller
2. ALFRED Lord Tennyson
3. The HUDSON and the East
4. George BENSON
5. Peter PARKER

Quizlink = Names of television BUTLERS or CHAUFFEURS (Max was the chauffeur in *Hart to Hart*; Alfred was the butler in *Batman*; Hudson was the butler in *Upstairs, Downstairs*; Benson was the butler in *Soap*; and Parker was Lady Penelope's chauffeur in *Thunderbirds*)

Round 6
1. GEORGE Eliot
2. *The MALTESE Falcon*
3. IRON Horse
4. VICTORIA Cannon
5. LATIN America

                Quizlink = Types of CROSS

Game 17 — Rounds 1–3

Round 1
1. Which terrorist group was responsible for the deaths of 11 competitors at the 1972 Olympic Games in Munich?
2. Which song was a number 1 hit for Pilot?
3. Who was the lead guitarist with the group Queen?
4. Who won an Oscar for his portrayal of Dr Jekyll and Mr Hyde?
5. Who played the wife of Terry Scott on television?

Round 2
1. Who played the short guy in the film *The Tall Guy*?
2. Which day follows Shrove Tuesday?
3. Which of the *Blue Peter* pets was replaced by Kari and Oki?
4. Which was the Beatles' own record label?
5. In which suburb was the Crossroads motel situated in the now defunct television soap *Crossroads*?

Round 3
1. What is the state capital of New Mexico?
2. On which river does the Italian city of Turin stand?
3. Which song was a hit for both the Beatles and Ferry Aid?
4. What was the nickname of tennis great Maureen Connolly?
5. Which song was Dooley Wilson asked to play in the film *Casablanca*?

Game 17 — Rounds 1–3

Round 1
1. Black SEPTEMBER
2. 'JANUARY'
3. Brian MAY
4. Fredric MARCH
5. JUNE Whitfield

              Quizlink = MONTHS of the year

Round 2
1. ROWAN Atkinson
2. ASH Wednesday
3. WILLOW
4. APPLE
5. Kings OAK

              Quizlink = TREES

Round 3
1. Santa FE
2. The River PO
3. 'Let it BE'
4. Little MO
5. 'AS Time Goes By'

    Quizlink = CHEMICAL SYMBOLS (Fe is the symbol for iron; Po for polonium; Be for beryllium; Mo for Molybdenum; and As for arsenic)

Game 17 — Rounds 4–6

Round 4
1 Which African country has a capital city called Nouackchott?
2 What symbol is on the back of a UK two pence coin?
3 Which character has been played on television by both Richard Greene and Jason Connery?
4 What was the occupation of Clint Eastwood in the film *For a Few Dollars More*?
5 In which 1981 film starring Sylvester Stallone and Michael Caine do Allied prisoners of war play their German captors at football?

Round 5
1 Which general was killed at Khartoum in 1885?
2 Who painted the ceiling of the Sistine Chapel?
3 Who said that he had come to bury Caesar, not to praise him?
4 Which grandma became a well-known US painter?
5 Which Spanish hero had the real name Rodrigo Diaz de Vivar?

Round 6
1 Which planet in our solar system takes over 247 years to orbit the Sun?
2 Which blonde actress appeared in the 1985 television series *CATS Eyes*?
3 What was the name of Benny Hill's milkman?
4 Besides heat, what is always created when you mix an alkali and an acid?
5 What was the nickname of the character with the surname O'Reilly in the television show M*A*S*H*?

Game 17 — Rounds 4–6

Round 4
1. MAURETANIA
2. PRINCE OF WALES feathers
3. Robin HOOD
4. BOUNTY hunter
5. *Escape to VICTORY*

Quizlink = Names of famous SHIPS

Round 5
1. GENERAL GORDON
2. MICHAELANGELO
3. MARC ANTONY
4. MOSES
5. EL CID

Quizlink = All have been played in films by CHARLTON HESTON

Round 6
1. PLUTO
2. Leslie ASH
3. ERNIE
4. SALT
5. RADAR

Quizlink = Words that are ACRONYMS (words composed of the initial letters of other words; PLUTO stands for Pipe Line Under The Ocean; ASH is for Action on Smoking and Health; ERNIE is the machine that draws the winning premium bond numbers and stands for Electronic Random Number Indicating Equipment; SALT means Strategic Arms Limitation Talks; and RADAR stands for Radio Detection and Ranging)

Game 18 — Rounds 1–3

Round 1
1 Which film starred Frank Sinatra as a drug addict?
2 Which TV quiz show is hosted by Nicky Campbell and Carol Smillie?
3 What was the invention of the British scientist Joseph Swan?
4 For which film did Gary Cooper win his second Oscar?
5 Which song was a number 3 hit for Status Quo in 1977?

Round 2
1 Which is the world's fastest moving land animal?
2 Which group sang 'I'm the Urban Spaceman' in 1968?
3 Which French monarch was married to Marie Antoinette?
4 On which river does the city of Glasgow stand?
5 Which British boxer was world junior lightweight champion in 1981?

Round 3
1 What was the title of the first Top 10 hit for the group Simply Red?
2 Which word, more often used in Scotland, describes a small plot of land adjoining a house which is worked by the house owner?
3 Who on television played the private investigator Jim Rockford?
4 Which duo had a 1978 Top 10 hit with the song 'Dancing in the City'?
5 Which character was played on television by Lorna Patterson and on film by Goldie Hawn?

Game 18 — Rounds 1–3

Round 1
1 *The Man With the Golden ARM*
2 *WHEEL of Fortune*
3 The ELECTRIC lamp
4 *HIGH Noon*
5 'ROCKING all over the World'

                Quizlink = Types of CHAIR

Round 2
1 The CHEETAH
2 BONZO Dog Doo Dah Band
3 LOUIS XVI
4 The River CLYDE
5 CORNELIUS Boza-Edwards

Quizlink = Names of film APES (Cheetah was the chimpanzee in the *Tarzan* films; Bonzo appeared in films such as *Bedtime for Bonzo* with Ronald Reagan; Louis was king of the apes in *The Jungle Book*; Clyde appeared in the *Any Which Way* films with Clint Eastwood; and Cornelius was one of the apes in the *Planet of the Apes* films)

Round 3
1 'HOLDING Back the Years'
2 CROFT
3 James GARNER
4 MARSHALL Hain
5 Private BENJAMIN

            Quizlink = Surnames of West Indian
            CRICKETERS or FAST BOWLERS

Game 18 — Rounds 4–6

Round 4
1 Who was famous for his lavish musicals featuring ornate dance routines with large numbers of dancers?
2 Which man-made construction connects the Pacific and Atlantic Oceans?
3 What is the name of Britain's most poisonous type of mushroom?
4 During which 1854 battle did the famous Charge of the Light Brigade occur?
5 What name is given to a low-roofed concrete emplacement for a machine gun or antitank gun?

Round 5
1 What is the name of the journal produced especially for the medical profession?
2 Which group had the original hit with the song 'Love Don't Live Here Anymore'?
3 Which 1971 film starring Gene Hackman won the Best Picture Oscar?
4 Which stretch of water washes the coasts of Northern Spain and Western France?
5 Who was known as 'the IT girl'?

Round 6
1 Who was the Wimbledon men's singles champion in 1987?
2 Which was the last play published by Joe Orton before his death in 1967?
3 Which was the only number 1 hit for the group Lieutenant Pigeon?
4 Which Carla Lane TV show features the character Freddy Boswell?
5 Which TV show featured the character Bradley Hardacre?

Game 18 — Rounds 4–6

Round 4
1. BUSBY Berkeley
2. The PANAMA Canal
3. The death CAP mushroom
4. The Battle of BALACLAVA
5. A PILLBOX

                Quizlink = Types of HATS

Round 5
1. *The LANCET*
2. ROSE Royce
3. *The FRENCH Connection*
4. The BAY of Biscay
5. Clara BOW

                Quizlink = Types of WINDOWS

Round 6
1. Pat CASH
2. *LOOT*
3. 'Mouldy Old DOUGH'
4. *BREAD*
5. *BRASS*

                Quizlink = Slang words for MONEY

Game 19 — Rounds 1-3

Round 1
1. Which literary character was referred to as 'the fat owl of the remove'?
2. Who in history reputedly singed the king of Spain's beard?
3. Which character in literature was bullied by Flashman?
4. What is the more common name of the star called Sirius?
5. What is the name of the rounded loaf of bread with a cross in the top?

Round 2
1. Which well-known US actor played the title role in the 1960 film *Spartacus*?
2. Who wrote *The Cherry Orchard*?
3. Which sea, part of the Western Pacific, lies between Borneo and the central Philippines?
4. Which US pianist and composer is credited with creating the style of music known as ragtime?
5. Who published *The Commonsense Book of Baby and Child Care* in 1946?

Round 3
1. Who won Britain's only athletics medal during the Montreal Olympics of 1976?
2. Which US president succeeded John F Kennedy?
3. What was the title of Bob Hoskins's animated box office hit of 1988?
4. Which Scottish physicist is credited with the invention of radar?
5. What was the name of the female character who was taught to speak properly in the film *My Fair Lady*?

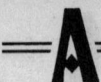

Game 19 — Rounds 1–3

Round 1
1. BILLY Bunter
2. Sir Francis DRAKE
3. TOM Brown
4. The DOG star
5. COB

Quizlink = Names for MALE ANIMALS

Round 2
1. KIRK Douglas
2. Anton CHEKHOV
3. SULU Sea
4. SCOTT Joplin
5. Benjamin SPOCK

Quizlink = Characters from the TV show *STAR TREK*

Round 3
1. Brendan FOSTER
2. Lyndon B JOHNSON
3. *WHO Framed Roger Rabbit*
4. Robert WATSON-Watt
5. Eliza DOLITTLE

Quizlink = Names of famous DOCTORS (of fact and fiction)

Game 19 — Rounds 4–6

Round 4
1 Who was British prime minister from 1955–57?
2 Who was the female star of the film *Gregory's Girl*?
3 Who was Bonnie Parker's infamous partner?
4 Who was the little girl who lived in *The Old Curiosity Shop*?
5 Who played Crockett in the television show *Miami Vice*?

Round 5
1 Which Alfred Hitchcock film starred James Stewart and Kim Novak?
2 Which is the nearest planet to the Sun?
3 Which stage in the life cycle of a butterfly follows the pupa?
4 Which company advertised itself as 'simply years ahead'?
5 At which game were Short and Kasparov in opposition in 1993?

Round 6
1 Which US actress received an Academy Award nomination for her role in the 1983 film *Terms of Endearment*?
2 Which US cop was played on television by William Shatner?
3 Where, according to the title of the first of the series, did Marty McFly go?
4 Which novel by Jules Verne features the character Professor Challenger?
5 What is the name given to the function on an electronic recording device, such as a videocassette or tape player, that permits rapid advancement of the tape?

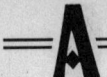

Game 19 — Rounds 4–6

Round 4
1. Anthony EDEN (accept the Earl of AVON)
2. DEE Hepburn
3. CLYDE Barrow
4. Nell TRENT
5. DON Johnson

    Quizlink = Names of British RIVERS

Round 5
1. *VERTIGO*
2. MERCURY
3. CHRYSALIS
4. PHILIPS
5. CHESS

    Quizlink = Names of RECORD LABELS

Round 6
1. Debra WINGER
2. T J HOOKER
3. *BACK To the Future*
4. *Journey to the CENTRE of the Earth*
5. Fast FORWARD

    Quizlink = Positions in the game of RUGBY

Game 20 — Rounds 1–3

Round 1

1. Which 'game' involves a number of people placing a single bullet in the barrel of a revolver, spinning the chamber and taking it in turns to point the gun at their head and pull the trigger?
2. In which Irish county is the town of Ennis?
3. In which television series did James Bolam star as Jack Ford?
4. Which Rider Haggard novel tells the story of an African queen who holds the secret of eternal life?
5. Which character got married in a 1786 Mozart opera?

Round 2

1. What is the name of the comedy actress who plays Blunderwoman to Russ Abbot's Cooperman?
2. Who played Douglas Bader in the film *Reach for the Sky*?
3. What was the title of Barbra Streisand's 1980 number 1 hit?
4. Who was the Manchester United player who was voted European footballer of the year in 1968?
5. Which television comedy show starred Richard O'Sullivan and Tim Brooke-Taylor?

Round 3

1. Which 1968 film won Katharine Hepburn her third Oscar?
2. Who wrote the novel *Kane and Abel*?
3. Which actress played Sybil Fawlty on TV?
4. What was the title of Madonna's second British Top 10 hit?
5. What name is given to the modern crime of driving motor vehicles through shop windows in order to steal from them?

Game 20 — Rounds 1–3

Round 1
1. Russian ROULETTE
2. CLARE
3. *WHEN the Boat Comes In*
4. *SHE*
5. FIGARO

Quizlink = Titles of
NUMBER 1 HIT SONGS

Round 2
1. BELLA Emberg
2. Kenneth MORE
3. 'A WOMAN in Love'
4. George BEST
5. *ME and My Girl*

Quizlink = Titles of
WOMEN'S MAGAZINES

Round 3
1. *The LION in Winter*
2. Jeffrey ARCHER
3. Prunella SCALES
4. 'Like a VIRGIN'
5. RAM raiding

Quizlink = Words describing
SIGNS OF THE ZODIAC

Game 20 — Rounds 4–6

Round 4

1. Which singer had a Top 10 hit with the song 'I Remember Elvis Presley'?
2. In which film did Frank Sinatra play a US officer in charge of a group of escaped prisoners of war?
3. Whom, according to Abraham Lincoln, can you not fool all of the time?
4. What was the name given to the medieval protection consisting of riveted metal links or rings?
5. In which film have Janet Gaynor, Judy Garland, and Barbra Streisand all played the lead role?

Round 5

1. Who wrote the novel *The Prisoner of Zenda*?
2. Which trophy is contested annually between the English league champions and the cup holders as a curtain raiser to the new football season?
3. Which group had the 1961 hit 'Pasadena'?
4. Who played the character Sir Lancelot Spratt in the *Doctor* series of films with Dirk Bogarde?
5. What was the title of rock star John Bon Jovi's 1993 album?

Round 6

1. Who rode Aldaniti to victory in the Grand National?
2. What was the nationality of United Nations secretary general U Thant?
3. Which organization has its HQ at Baden Powell House?
4. What did Judas Iscariot receive as payment for his betrayal of Jesus?
5. In which European city can you see the Little Mermaid?

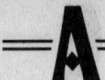

Game 20 — Rounds 4-6

Round 4
1. Danny MIRROR
2. *Von Ryan's EXPRESS*
3. All of the PEOPLE
4. Chain MAIL (or just MAIL)
5. *A STAR is Born*

Quizlink = NEWSPAPERS

Round 5
1. Anthony HOPE
2. The CHARITY Shield
3. The TEMPERANCE Seven
4. James Robertson JUSTICE
5. *Keep the FAITH*

Quizlink = Five of the seven traditional VIRTUES

Round 6
1. Bob CHAMPION
2. BURMESE
3. The SCOUT Association
4. 30 pieces of SILVER
5. COPENHAGEN

Quizlink = Names of famous HORSES (from fact or fiction)
(Champion was the name of singing cowboy Gene Autrey's horse; Burmese was ridden by HM Queen Elizabeth II at several state functions; Scout and Silver belonged to Tonto and the Lone Ranger respectively; and Copenhagen was ridden by the Duke of Wellington at the Battle of Waterloo in 1815)

Game 21 — Rounds 1-3

Round 1

1. Which couple were played on television by Michael Crawford and Michelle Dotrice?
2. Who is the most famous of English lexicographers?
3. Who played the title role in the film *Whatever Happened to Baby Jane*?
4. Which British historian wrote *The Origins of the Second World War*?
5. Which professor was created by George Bernard Shaw in his play *Pygmalion*?

Round 2

1. Who in 1978 married Marie-Christine von Reibnitz?
2. In which thoroughfare is the great fire of London thought to have started?
3. According to the Bible, who committed the world's first murder?
4. Who was assassinated in Memphis in April 1968?
5. Who was captain of the Warwickshire cricket team which in 1994 narrowly failed to achieve the grand slam of all four major trophies?

Round 3

1. What was the profession of Eddie Felson, the character played by Paul Newman in the film *The Hustler*?
2. Which horse was champion hurdler in 1980 and 1981?
3. Which actress starred opposite Alan Ladd in the film *The Blue Dahlia*?
4. Which singer had a hit in the British charts with the song 'Love Really Hurts Without You'?
5. Which US actor died at the age of 22 after collapsing outside a Hollywood night-club in Oct 1993?

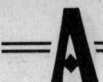

Game 21 — Rounds 1–3

Round 1
1. Frank and Betty SPENCER
2. Samuel JOHNSON
3. Bette DAVIS
4. A J P TAYLOR
5. Henry HIGGINS

Quizlink = Surnames of World SNOOKER CHAMPIONS

Round 2
1. Prince Michael of KENT
2. Pudding LANE
3. CAIN (who murdered his brother Abel)
4. Martin LUTHER King
5. Dermot REEVE

Quizlink = SUPERMAN (Clark Kent was the alias used by Superman while working for the *Daily Planet* newspaper where Lois Lane also worked. Dean Cain plays the TV Superman and Christopher Reeve played the film version. Lex Luther is Superman's sworn enemy)

Round 3
1. He was a POOL player
2. SEA Pigeon
3. Veronica LAKE
4. Billy OCEAN
5. RIVER Phoenix

Quizlink = Terms for bodies of WATER

Game 21 — Rounds 4–6

Round 4
1. What is the name of the dog in 'the Perishers' newspaper strip cartoon?
2. In *Treasure Island* what was *Hispaniola*?
3. Which Fred Astaire film features the song 'Cheek to Cheek'?
4. What has the chemical symbol Fe?
5. In the Stephen King novel *Christine*, what was Christine?

Round 5
1. What is the name of the substance consisting of compacted talc which is used by tailors for marking cloth?
2. Which cocktail consists of Tia Maria, vodka, and coke?
3. What is the name of the type of sale where the price of an article is reduced until somebody agrees to buy it?
4. What was the nickname of opera singer Jenny Lind?
5. What name is given to the practice, popular at sporting events, whereby a rippling effect is created by the audience standing in sequence with arms raised, then sitting down?

Round 6
1. Which television quiz/game show was hosted by Gordon Burns?
2. In which film did Cary Grant play the nephew of two murderous old ladies?
3. From which venue was a Sunday night show presented weekly by Tommy Trinder and Bruce Forsyth among others?
4. Who was the lead singer with the group Queen?
5. What do people in the USA call a 5 cent coin?

Game 21 — Rounds 4–6

Round 4
1. BOOT
2. SHIP
3. *TOP HAT*
4. IRON
5. CAR

Quizlink = Playing pieces in the board game MONOPOLY

Round 5
1. FRENCH chalk
2. Black RUSSIAN
3. DUTCH auction
4. The SWEDISH Nightingale
5. MEXICAN wave

Quizlink = NATIONALITIES

Round 6
1. *The KRYPTON Factor*
2. *ARSENIC and Old Lace*
3. The London PALLADIUM
4. Freddie MERCURY
5. NICKEL

Quizlink = Names of CHEMICAL ELEMENTS

Game 22 — Rounds 1–3

Round 1
1 Who is Fred Flintstone's next-door neighbour?
2 What name is given to a person who practises yoga?
3 Which is the main London station serving the West Country?
4 Who became famous as television's Maigret?
5 Which character in *The Mikado* was Lord High Everything Else?

Round 2
1 Where is bile stored in the human body?
2 Which author had the real name Charles Dodgson?
3 In which London thoroughfare did Sherlock Holmes live?
4 Who became Britain's first ever Labour prime minister in 1924?
5 Who played the character Barbara Good in a long running BBC show?

Round 3
1 Which German magazine published excerpts from what it claimed were the personal diaries of Adolf Hitler, though they were ultimately proved to be fakes?
2 Which football club is nicknamed 'the Tigers'?
3 Which song was a hit for both Max Bygraves and Wink Martindale?
4 What name is given to the fruit of forest trees such as the beech, which is used as fodder for pigs?
5 Which antislavery novel by Harriet Beecher Stowe features the evil Simon Legree?

Game 22 — Rounds 1–3

Round 1
1. BARNEY Rubble
2. YOGI
3. PADDINGTON
4. RUPERT Davies
5. POOH-Bah

            Quizlink = Names of famous
                   fictional BEARS

Round 2
1. The GALL bladder
2. LEWIS Carroll
3. BAKER Street
4. James Ramsey MACDONALD
5. Felicity KENDAL

            Quizlink = Surnames of television
                   NEWS READERS

Round 3
1. *STERN*
2. HULL City
3. 'DECK of Cards'
4. MAST
5. *Uncle Tom's CABIN*

            Quizlink = Parts of a SHIP

Game 22 — Rounds 4–6

Round 4
1 What is the state capital of Ohio?
2 Who created the character Jay Gatsby?
3 What was the job of Long John Silver aboard the *Hispaniola*?
4 Where can you see the riding track called Rotten Row?
5 Which politician has been referred to as 'Red Ken'?

Round 5
1 Which were the first four words broadcast from the surface of the Moon in 1969?
2 Which BBC show takes up the cases of convicted criminals it believes have had a raw deal from the legal system?
3 Who is the US equivalent of Alf Garnett?
4 Which conductor founded the Promenade Concerts?
5 Which song did the Tweets take to number 2 in the charts in 1981?

Round 6
1 Who played the character Joe Sugden in the TV soap *Emmerdale*?
2 Who had a hit with the song 'In the Midnight Hour'?
3 The greatest wicket keeper of his era, he played test cricket for England between the years of 1946 and 1959. He holds the record for the longest time at the crease before scoring a run, achieved when he spent an astonishing 95 minutes at the wicket before getting off the mark against Australia in 1947. Who is he?
4 What was the name of the crew's pet cat in the original *Alien!* film?
5 Which New Zealand athlete was the first to break the 3 minutes and 50 seconds barrier for the mile?

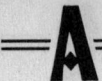 **Game 22 — Rounds 4–6**

Round 4
1. COLUMBUS
2. F SCOTT Fitzgerald
3. He was the ship's COOK
4. Hyde PARK
5. Ken LIVINGSTONE

   Quizlink = Surnames of famous EXPLORERS (Christopher Columbus; Robert Falcon Scott; James Cook; Mungo Park; and David Livingstone)

Round 5
1. 'The EAGLE has landed'
2. *ROUGH Justice*
3. Archie BUNKER
4. Sir Henry WOOD
5. 'The BIRDIE Song'

   Quizlink = Terms used in the game of GOLF

Round 6
1. FRASER Hines
2. WILSON Pickett
3. GODFREY Evans
4. JONES
5. John WALKER

   Quizlink = Surnames of the regular members of *DAD'S ARMY* under the command of Captain Mainwaring in the television comedy series

Game 23 — Rounds 1–3

Round 1
1. Which short story by the German author Thomas Mann became a film starring Dirk Bogarde?
2. What is the name given to the supposed burial gown of Jesus Christ?
3. What was the name of the girl in the children's television puppet show *The Magic Roundabout*?
4. How are the characters Valentine and Proteus referred to in the title of the play in which they are the central characters?
5. Which private eye did Frank Sinatra play on film?

Round 2
1. What was the popular name given to the universally unpopular forerunner to council tax?
2. What name is given to a small crown worn by a prince or a peer?
3. Which singer had a 1978 hit with the song 'Lovely Day'?
4. Where did television policeman George Dixon work?
5. Which condition usually affecting children is characterized by a harsh cough and difficulty in breathing?

Round 3
1. Which character did Doris Speed play in *Coronation Street*?
2. Who was the female star of the film *A Fish Called Wanda*?
3. Who won six world snooker championships during the 1980s?
4. Who was known as 'The Wizard of Dribble'?
5. Which is the best known of the creations of Reverend W Awdry?

Game 23 — Rounds 1–3

Round 1
1. 'Death in VENICE'
2. The Shroud of TURIN
3. FLORENCE
4. *Two Gentlemen of VERONA*
5. Tony ROME

                Quizlink = ITALIAN CITIES

Round 2
1. The POLL tax
2. CORONET
3. Bill WITHERS
4. DOCK Green (in the early TV show starring Jack Warner)
5. CROUP

                Quizlink = Parts of a HORSE

Round 3
1. Annie WALKER
2. Jamie Lee CURTIS
3. Steve DAVIS
4. STANLEY Matthews
5. THOMAS the Tank Engine

                Quizlink = SPORTING CUPS (the Walker and Curtis Cups are awarded for golf; the Davis Cup for tennis; the Stanley Cup for ice hockey; and the Thomas Cup for badminton)

Game 23 — Rounds 4–6

Round 4

1. Which river runs along the border between Argentina and Uruguay?
2. Which sporting trophy did Real Madrid win for the first five years of its existence?
3. What term is often used (because of its shape) to describe a UFO or a spacecraft believed to be from another planet?
4. What is the name given to the annual football game played between the winners of the AFL and the winners of the NFL in the USA?
5. 'Smoke Gets in Your Eyes' was a 1959 number 1 hit for which group?

Round 5

1. Which hero of classical mythology is known for performing 12 labours?
2. With which athletic event is the Finnish competitor Tina Lillak associated?
3. What is the name of the three-pronged fork traditionally carried by Britannia?
4. What was the name of the Roman god of fire?
5. What is the nickname of snooker player Alex Higgins?

Round 6

1. Which Greek singer had her only British hit with the song 'Only Love' in 1986?
2. What name is given to a hand in the card game poker consisting of the five highest value cards in a single suit?
3. In the Shakespeare play *Twelfth Night*, what is the name of Olivia's hard-drinking uncle?
4. Which singer had a 1983 Top 10 hit with 'Bird of Paradise'?
5. Which British golfer won the British Open in 1985?

Game 23 — Rounds 4–6

Round 4
1. The River PLATE
2. The European CUP
3. Flying SAUCER
4. Super BOWL
5. The PLATTERS

Quizlink = Items of
CROCKERY

Round 5
1. HERCULES
2. JAVELIN
3. TRIDENT
4. VULCAN
5. HURRICANE

Quizlink = Makes of
AIRCRAFT

Round 6
1. NANA Mouskouri
2. Royal FLUSH
3. Sir TOBY Belch
4. SNOWY White
5. SANDY Lyle

Quizlink = Names of famous DOGS (Nana was the name of the dog in *Peter Pan*; Flush belonged to Elizabeth Barrett Browning; Toby features in a traditional Punch and Judy show; Snowy is Tin Tin's dog; and Sandy belonged to Little Orphan Annie)

Game 24 — Rounds 1–3

Round 1
1. In literature, what was the real name of the man known as the Scarlet Pimpernel?
2. In which film of the 1980s did Dudley Moore play the part of an elf?
3. Who was the commander of *Stingray* in the television puppet series of the same name?
4. What did Jason and the Argonauts go in search of?
5. Which Panamanian boxer defeated Sugar Ray Leonard in a world title fight?

Round 2
1. Which county has its administrative headquarters in Middlesbrough?
2. Which female singer had a 1978 Top 10 hit with the song 'We're All Alone'?
3. Who was the director of the FBI from 1924 until his death in 1972?
4. What is a bird in the hand proverbially said to be worth?
5. Who wrote the story of Rip van Winkle?

Round 3
1. Who composed the 'Trumpet Voluntary'?
2. Which US singer sang 'Uptown Girl'?
3. Which Englishman has been British squash champion on six occasions?
4. Who wrote about the adventures of Robinson Crusoe?
5. What is the name of the ancient cat in *Old Possum's Book of Practical Cats* by T S Eliot?

Game 24 — Rounds 1–3

Round 1
1. Sir Percy BLAKENEY
2. *SANTA CLAUS the Movie*
3. TROY Tempest
4. The GOLDEN FLEECE
5. ROBERTO Duran

>Quizlink = Names of
>DERBY-WINNING HORSES

Round 2
1. CLEVELAND
2. Rita COOLIDGE
3. J Edgar HOOVER
4. Two in the BUSH
5. WASHINGTON Irving

>Quizlink = Surnames of PRESIDENTS of the USA (Grover Cleveland; Calvin Coolidge; Herbert Hoover; George Bush; George Washington)

Round 3
1. JEREMIAH Clark
2. Billy JOEL
3. JONAH Barrington
4. DANIEL Defoe
5. Old DEUTERONOMY

>Quizlink = BOOKS OF
>THE BIBLE

Game 24 — Rounds 4–6

Round 4
1 Who was the female star of the television mini series *The Thorn Birds*?
2 Which former Egyptian obelisk now stands on the north bank of the River Thames?
3 Outside which building in Hollywood do film stars traditionally leave their hand and footprints?
4 Which well-known television character was originally played by William Hartnell?
5 In which 1992 film does Whoopi Goldberg play a gangster's moll who masquerades as a nun?

Round 5
1 Which 17th-century work tells of Christian's travels from the City of Destruction to the Celestial City?
2 Where was Daniel imprisoned, according to the Bible?
3 Snowy, tawny, and barn are examples of which creatures?
4 Which film was voted Best Picture at the Academy Award ceremony of 1990?
5 By what name is the Society of Friends alternatively known?

Round 6
1 Who played Horace Rumpole on television?
2 Which building is the official residence of HM Queen Elizabeth the Queen Mother?
3 Which British actress, the wife of Charles Laughton, starred in the 1957 film *Witness For the Prosecution*?
4 What is the traditional flavour-enhancing accompaniment to a fish dish?
5 Which US stand-up comedian was the subject of a Dustin Hoffman film?

Game 24 — Rounds 4–6

Round 4
1. Rachel WARD
2. Cleopatra's NEEDLE
3. Graumann's Chinese THEATRE
4. DOCTOR Who
5. *SISTER Act*

>Quizlink = Things you might
>see in a HOSPITAL

Round 5
1. *PILGRIM'S Progress* by John Bunyan
2. The LION'S den
3. OWLS
4. *Dances With WOLVES*
5. QUAKERS

>Quizlink = NICKNAMES of English FOOTBALL TEAMS
>(Pilgrims = Plymouth Argyle; Lions = Millwall; Owls =
>Sheffield Wednesday; Wolves = Wolverhampton Wanderers;
>Quakers = Darlington)

Round 6
1. LEO McKern
2. CLARENCE House
3. ELSA Lanchester
4. PARSLEY sauce
5. LENNY Bruce

>Quizlink = Names of
>famous LIONS

Game 25 — Rounds 1–3

Round 1
1 What is the name of the hospital situated near Newcastle-upon-Tyne that specializes in heart and lung surgery?
2 Which London thoroughfare is noted for its high quality tailors?
3 Which football club did Kenny Dalglish manage to the Premiership title in 1995?
4 What was the name of the establishment run by Anthony Perkins in the film *Psycho*?
5 Who was the pilot of *Flyer 1* during the world's first ever powered flight at Kittyhawk in 1903?

Round 2
1 Who was the author of *Gulliver's Travels*?
2 Who wrote the novel *Beau Geste*?
3 According to the author A A Milne, which young boy went with Alice to see the changing of the guard at Buckingham Palace?
4 Which political commentator has presented both *Weekend World* and *A Week in Politics*?
5 What was the nickname of French singer Edith Piaf?

Round 3
1 Since the Bolshevik execution of Czar Nicholas II of Russia and his family in 1918, several women have claimed to be his daughter. What was her name?
2 Who played faded film star Norma Desmond in the 1950 film *Sunset Boulevard*?
3 Which song was a number 1 hit for Esther and Abi Ofarim?
4 Who played the part of Edith, wife of cafe owner Rene, in the television comedy series *'Allo 'Allo*?
5 What was the name of the Thracian slave who led an ultimately unsuccessful gladiator revolt against Rome in 73 BC?

Game 25 — Rounds 1–3

Round 1
1. FREEMAN hospital
2. SAVILE Row
3. BLACKBURN Rovers
4. The BATES Motel
5. Orville WRIGHT

   Quizlink = Surnames of DISC JOCKEYS
   (all formerly of Radio 1)

Round 2
1. Jonathan SWIFT
2. P C WREN
3. Christopher ROBIN
4. Peter JAY
5. 'The Little SPARROW'

   Quizlink = Names of BIRDS

Round 3
1. ANASTASIA
2. GLORIA Swanson
3. 'CINDERELLA, Rockerfella'
4. CARMEN Silvera
5. SPARTACUS

   Quizlink = Titles of BALLETS (Anastasia was by Martinu; Gloria by Poulenc; Cinderella by Prokofiev; Carmen by Bizet; and Spartacus by Khachaturian)

Game 25 — Rounds 4–6

Round 4
1. Which is the world's largest car manufacturing company?
2. Which was the only horse to beat the great Mill Reef on English soil?
3. What is the name of the yellow playing piece in the board game Cluedo?
4. What was the title of the play written by Noel Coward in 1930?
5. Whose first cabinet post was as chief secretary to the Treasury in 1987?

Round 5
1. Which title was relinquished by politician Tony Benn?
2. Which song title was a hit for both Tracy Ullman and the Beach Boys?
3. What is a rockhopper?
4. Which film tells the story of a group of Australian schoolgirls who go on a day trip and are never seen again?
5. Which television show features the Sunshine Cab company?

Round 6
1. Which man, who shares his name with a famous college, invented today's most popular type of lock?
2. Who played the character Templeton Peck in the television adventure show *The A Team*?
3. Who starred in the films *12 O'clock High* and *The Yearling*?
4. Which town is situated at the northern tip of mainland Britain?
5. What was the title of the only chart entry for the Bonzo Dog Doo Dah Band?

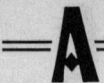 ## Game 25 — Rounds 4–6

Round 4
1. GENERAL Motors
2. BRIGADIER Gerard
3. COLONEL Mustard
4. PRIVATE Lives
5. John MAJOR

                Quizlink = ARMY RANKS

Round 5
1. VISCOUNT Stansgate
2. 'BREAKAWAY'
3. It is a type of PENGUIN
4. *PICNIC at Hanging Rock*
5. *TAXI*

                Quizlink = Names of CHOCOLATE
                      bars or biscuits

Round 6
1. LINUS Yale
2. Dirk BENEDICT
3. GREGORY Peck
4. JOHN O'Groats
5. 'I'm the URBAN Spaceman'

                Quizlink = Names adopted by POPES

Game 26 — Rounds 1–3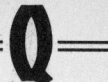

Round 1
1 Which group had a number 1 hit with 'In the Summertime'?
2 Who wrote and starred in the 1976 film *Rocky*?
3 In falconry, what is the name of the short leather strap permanently attached to the leg of a bird, which can be used as a leash?
4 Who founded the film company whose films are always preceded by an athlete banging a huge gong?
5 Who won three British Open golf championships during the 1980s?

Round 2
1 Which Daphne du Maurier novel was made into a 1944 film starring Basil Rathbone and Joan Fontaine?
2 What was the title of the first number 1 hit for the Shadows?
3 What is the state capital of Wyoming?
4 As a dog is canine, which creature is corvine?
5 Which horse did Lester Pigott ride to victory in the 1984 St Leger?

Round 3
1 Which actress played Pam Ewing in the television show *Dallas*?
2 What name is given to the head of a community of nuns?
3 Which Charlotte Brontë heroine became a governess at Thornfield Hall?
4 Of which Canadian province is Toronto the capital city?
5 What is the more common name given to the constellation Ursa Major?

Game 26 — Rounds 1–3

Round 1
1. MUNGO JERRY
2. SYLVESTER Stallone
3. It is called a JESS
4. J ARTHUR Rank
5. TOM Watson

Quizlink = Names of famous CATS (Mungo Jerry is from *Old Possum's Book of Practical Cats*; Sylvester chases Tweety Pie; Jess is Postman Pat's cat; Arthur advertised cat food on television; and Tom is the sworn enemy of Jerry mouse)

Round 2
1. *Frenchman's CREEK*
2. 'APACHE'
3. CHEYENNE
4. CROW
5. COMANCHE Run

Quizlink = Names of AMERICAN INDIAN TRIBES

Round 3
1. VICTORIA Principal
2. Mother SUPERIOR
3. Jane EYRE
4. ONTARIO
5. The GREAT BEAR

Quizlink = Names of well-known LAKES

Game 26 — Rounds 4–6

Round 4

1. Which author created the character Tarzan?
2. Who was the well-known co-writer of Richard Rogers who collaborated with him on musicals such as *South Pacific* and *The Sound of Music*?
3. Who starred with Roger Moore in the television show *The Persuaders*?
4. Who is the jazz singer wife of musician Johnny Dankworth?
5. Who is the champagne-guzzling friend of Edina, played by Joanna Lumley in the television comedy show *Absolutely Fabulous*?

Round 5

1. Who is Nick Owen's co-presenter on the daytime television show *Good Morning*?
2. Which US author won the Pulitzer Prize for her novel *The Good Earth*?
3. Which television sci-fi show of the late 1970s and early 1980s starred Joanna Lumley and David Macallum as two of 115 'elements'?
4. In the story by Frank L Baum, in which city did *The Wonderful Wizard of Oz* reside?
5. A US singer/dancer of the 1930s with the real first name of Ethel, she appeared in musicals such as *Dames* and *42nd Street*. Who was she?

Round 6

1. Which well-known horror story was written by Robert Louis Stevenson?
2. A famous Russian author, he is considered the father of Russian literature. In 1902 *The Lower Depths*, the first and greatest of his 15 plays, was performed by the Moscow Art Theatre. Who was he?
3. Which general term is used to describe the countries situated between the southern border of the USA and the northern border of Colombia?
4. Who played the part of Spike in the television comedy show *Hi-de-Hi*?
5. Mary Tealby founded a 'temporary home for lost and starving dogs' in 1860. How is this home known today?

Game 26 — Rounds 4–6

Round 4
1. EDGAR Rice-Burroughs
2. OSCAR Hammerstein II
3. TONY Curtis
4. CLEO Laine
5. PATSY

Quizlink = AWARDS made in the USA (the Edgar is an award made for mystery writing; the Oscar for films; the Tony is awarded in the theatre; the Cleo for television commercials; and the Patsy for performances by animals)

Round 5
1. Anne DIAMOND
2. PEARL Buck
3. *SAPPHIRE and Steel*
4. The EMERALD City
5. RUBY Keeler

Quizlink = Names of PRECIOUS STONES

Round 6
1. *The Strange Case of Doctor Jekyll and Mr HYDE*
2. Maxim GORKY
3. CENTRAL America
4. Jeffrey HOLLAND
5. BATTERSEA Dogs' Home

Quizlink = Names of well-known PARKS

Game 27 — Rounds 1–3

Round 1

1. John Montagu invented a new type of food in the 1760s so that he did not have to leave the gaming tables. By what title was he known?
2. Which famous military conflict occurred close to England's south coast in 1066?
3. What is the title of the only novel written by the author J D Salinger?
4. According to the well-known wartime song, over what were there bluebirds?
5. Which 18th-century portrait painter produced over 50 portraits of Emma Hamilton in various guises?

Round 2

1. Of which province of South Africa is Bloemfontein the capital city?
2. Who was the central character in the film *The Third Man*?
3. Which television show hosted by Cilla Black introduces couples who have never met?
4. What is the nickname of New York City?
5. What is the name of Popeye's girlfriend?

Round 3

1. Whose last Top 10 hit in 1968 was 'Son of a Preacher Man'?
2. Who wrote the poem 'The Pied Piper of Hamelin'?
3. Which character did Stuart Damon play in the television sci-fi series *The Champions*?
4. Who was the last man to win three consecutive British Open golf championships?
5. What was the old Roman capital of England?

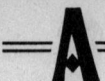# Game 27 — Rounds 1–3

Round 1
1. The Earl of SANDWICH
2. The Battle of HASTINGS
3. *The Catcher in the RYE*
4. 'The white cliffs of DOVER'
5. George ROMNEY

   Quizlink = Names of five of the seven CINQUE PORTS
   (the others are Winchelsea and Hythe)

Round 2
1. ORANGE Free State
2. Harry LIME
3. *Blind DATE*
4. The Big APPLE
5. OLIVE Oyl

   Quizlink = Names of FRUITS

Round 3
1. Dusty SPRINGFIELD
2. Robert BROWNING
3. Craig STIRLING
4. Peter THOMPSON
5. WINCHESTER

   Quizlink = Names associated with GUNS,
   WEAPONS, or FIREARMS

Game 27 — Rounds 4–6

Round 4
1. What is the name of the spoof reporter played on television by Steve Coogan?
2. What was the title of Tolkien's sequel to *The Hobbit*?
3. What do members of the House of Commons refer to as 'another place'?
4. What was the name of the group formed by the three female characters in the television show *Rock Follies*? The show starred Rula Lenska, Charlotte Cornwell, and Julie Covington.
5. Which group had a 1968 Top 10 hit with the song 'Green Tambourine'?

Round 5
1. What name is given to the wide expanse of coral located off the coast of Australia?
2. Which royal residence suffered serious damage due to a fire in Nov 1992?
3. In the game of cricket, which fielder stands closest to the wicket keeper's right hand when there is a right-handed batsman?
4. What is the name of the world-famous intersection formed by Broadway, Seventh Avenue, and 42nd Street in the city of New York?
5. Which variety of hard green-skinned apple is named after an Australian woman who died in 1870?

Round 6
1. Who was the famous royal fashion designer and dressmaker who died in 1979?
2. Which character from the original *Star Trek* television series was played by De Forest Kelly?
3. Who played the part of Piers Fletcher-Dervish, personal assistant to MP Alan B'stard, in the television comedy show *The New Statesman*?
4. Which Yorkshire-born soprano became a Dame in 1976?
5. Who played the Air Raid Patrol warden in the classic comedy show *Dad's Army*?

Game 27 — Rounds 4–6

Round 4
1. Alan PARTRIDGE
2. *The Lord of the RINGS*
3. The House of LORDS
4. The Little LADIES
5. The Lemon PIPERS

    Quizlink = Gifts brought by my true love in the song 'THE TWELVE DAYS OF CHRISTMAS'

Round 5
1. The Great Barrier REEF
2. WINDSOR Castle
3. First SLIP
4. Times SQUARE
5. GRANNY (Maria Ann) Smith

    Quizlink = Types of KNOTS

Round 6
1. Norman HARTNELL
2. Dr Leonard McCOY
3. Michael TROUGHTON
4. Janet BAKER
5. Bill PERTWEE

    Quizlink = Surnames of actors who have played DR WHO

Game 28 — Rounds 1-3

Round 1

1. Who, according to legend, cut the Gordian Knot?
2. Which British female athlete broke a world record in 1986 and became world champion the following year?
3. Which Swedish chemist invented dynamite?
4. Which group had chart hits entitled 'Green Onions' and 'Time is Tight'?
5. What name is given to the National Hunt horse racing meeting held annually in March in Gloucestershire, the centre piece of which is the Gold Cup Steeplechase?

Round 2

1. What is the name of the highest peak in England?
2. Which ventriloquist had a dummy called Lord Charles?
3. Which British classical guitarist is also a leading exponent of the lute?
4. What is the name of the hook-shaped sandy peninsula in southern Massachusetts popular as a tourist resort?
5. Who played the part of Bomber in the television series *Auf Wiedersehen Pet*?

Round 3

1. Which 1979 film won Oscars for both Dustin Hoffman and Meryl Streep?
2. Which is the highest mountain on the North American continent?
3. Which author created the characters Uncas and Hawkeye in his novel *The Last of the Mohicans*?
4. What name is given to a particular type of seaweed which has been fried as a breakfast food?
5. Which guitarist is probably best known for his album *Abraxas*?

Game 28 — Rounds 1–3

Round 1
1. ALEXANDER the Great
2. Fatima WHITBREAD
3. Alfred NOBEL
4. BOOKER T and the MGs
5. The CHELTENHAM Festival

Quizlink = Names of
LITERARY PRIZES or AWARDS

Round 2
1. Scafell PIKE
2. RAY Allan
3. Julian BREAM
4. Cape COD
5. Pat ROACH

Quizlink = Names of FISH

Round 3
1. *KRAMER Vs Kramer*
2. Mount McKINLEY
3. James Fenimore COOPER
4. LAVER bread
5. Carlos SANTANA

Quizlink = Surnames of post-war
WIMBLEDON CHAMPIONS (Jack Kramer; Chuck McKinley;
Ashley Cooper; Rod Laver; Manuel Santana)

Game 28 — Rounds 4–6

Round 4

1. Which actor played the part of James Bond's adversary, Jaws, in two films?
2. Which event prompted the resignation of Anthony Eden from his position as British prime minister in 1957?
3. Which country has land borders with Costa Rica and Colombia?
4. Which television detective of the 1980s was played by actor Lee Horsley?
5. Which British actor and scriptwriter starred in television's *Z Cars* and wrote the script for the 1979 film *Yanks*?

Round 5

1. Who was the first Lord Protector of England?
2. Which Welsh singer had a 1970 hit with the song 'Daughter of Darkness'?
3. Who was assassinated by members of her own bodyguard in 1984?
4. In the children's nursery rhyme 'Humpty Dumpty', who couldn't put Humpty together again?
5. Which US singer, popular in the early 1960s, had a British Top 10 hit with the song 'Devil Woman'?

Round 6

1. What is traditionally awarded to Olympic runners up?
2. Which British driver set a new world landspeed record in his jet-powered car *Thrust II*?
3. Which famous horse race was first contested in 1836 and won by a horse called the Duke?
4. Who was the male star of the film *Falling Down*?
5. Which veteran Texan oilman became an overnight celebrity when he and his team of trouble-shooters were called upon to extinguish the fire raging on the Piper Alpha oil platform in July 1988?

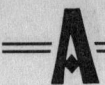 **Game 28 — Rounds 4–6**

Round 4
1. Richard KIEL
2. The SUEZ Crisis
3. PANAMA
4. Matt HOUSTON
5. Colin WELLAND

Quizlink = Names of important CANALS

Round 5
1. OLIVER Cromwell
2. TOM JONES
3. Indira GANDHI
4. 'All the king's horses and ALL THE KING'S MEN'
5. MARTY Robbins

Quizlink = Titles of
OSCAR-WINNING FILMS

Round 6
1. SILVER medal
2. Richard NOBLE
3. The GRAND National
4. Michael DOUGLAS
5. RED Adair

Quizlink = Species of FIR TREE

Game 29 — Rounds 1–3

Round 1
1 Which British athlete won two sprinting medals at the Moscow Olympic Games of 1980?
2 Who did Jane Eyre marry after working for him, in the novel by Charlotte Brontë?
3 Which flavouring is chiefly associated with the manufacturers Lea & Perrins?
4 Which famous person was assassinated by John Wilkes Booth in the USA in 1865?
5 Which female singer had her first British hit with the song 'Heaven is a Place on Earth' in 1987?

Round 2
1 By what name do we know the collection of Arabic stories including 'Aladdin' and 'Ali Baba' told by Scheherazade to her husband?
2 Which Australian actress better known for her stage work, appeared in the films *The Killing of Sister George* and *The Drowning Pool*?
3 Which US colonel was found guilty of three charges arising from the so-called 'Iran-Contragate' affair and fined $150,000?
4 The fifth film in the Harry Callaghan series starring Clint Eastwood was released in 1988. What was its title?
5 What was the title of Chris de Burgh's 1986 number 1 hit?

Round 3
1 Which horse slipped on the run in while leading the 1956 Grand National?
2 Which Australian entrepreneur organized a so-called 'Cricket Circus' in the 1970s?
3 Which boxer lost his world heavyweight title to Rocky Marciano in 1952?
4 Who did Ray Illingworth replace as chairman of England's cricket selectors?
5 Which football club replaced Barrow in the Football League in 1972?

Game 29 — Rounds 1-3

Round 1
1. Allan WELLS
2. Mr ROCHESTER
3. WORCESTER sauce
4. Abraham LINCOLN
5. Belinda CARLISLE

Quizlink = Names of
BRITISH CITIES

Round 2
1. *The ARABIAN Nights*
2. CORAL Browne
3. Oliver NORTH
4. *The DEAD Pool*
5. 'Lady in RED'

Quizlink = Names of SEAS

Round 3
1. DEVON Loch
2. KERRY Packer
3. JERSEY Joe Walcott
4. Ted DEXTER
5. HEREFORD United

Quizlink = Breeds of CATTLE

Game 29 — Rounds 4–6

Round 4

1 Which football club defeated Arsenal in the final of the 1972 FA Cup and were themselves beaten in the final the following year?
2 Which surgeon performed the world's first heart transplant in 1967?
3 Who played the part of Sergeant Major Williams in the television comedy series *It Ain't Half Hot Mum*?
4 Who was the female singer with the 1960s group the Seekers?
5 Which US singer's only British number 1 hit was 'It's Only Make Believe' in 1958?

Round 5

1 Which character did Robert Redford play in a successful western film of 1969?
2 Who became world light heavyweight boxing champion when he knocked out Britain's Freddie Mills in 1950?
3 What was the character name of television's *Fall Guy* played by Lee Majors?
4 What is the name of the small island south of the Isle of Man?
5 Which woman, who became the subject of a 1972 film, referred to Lord Byron as 'Mad, bad and dangerous to know'?

Round 6

1 Which square immediately precedes Whitechapel on a Monopoly board?
2 Who preceded Neil Kinnock as leader of the Labour Party?
3 Which war did Britain and Spain fight between the years of 1739 and 1741?
4 Which French jockey rode three English classic winners during the 1980s?
5 In which film did the character of Doc Emmet Brown first appear?

Game 29 — Rounds 4–6

Round 4

1. LEEDS United
2. Christiaan BARNARD
3. WINDSOR Davies
4. Judith DURHAM
5. CONWAY Twitty

> Quizlink = Names of well-known
> CASTLES

Round 5

1. The Sundance KID
2. JOEY Maxim
3. COLT Seevers
4. The CALF of Man
5. Lady Caroline LAMB

> Quizlink = Words describing
> YOUNG ANIMALS

Round 6

1. Community CHEST
2. Michael FOOT
3. The War of Jenkins's EAR
4. Freddie HEAD
5. *BACK to the Future*

> Quizlink = Parts of
> THE BODY

Game 30 — Rounds 1–3

Round 1
1. Who wrote the 18th-century novels *The Adventures of Peregrine Pickle* and *The Adventures of Roderick Random*?
2. In which film of 1966 did James Coburn play a US secret agent?
3. What is the name of the island shared by the countries of Haiti and the Dominican Republic?
4. What was the nickname of professional snooker player David Taylor?
5. Who played the commander of *HMS Compass Rose* in the film *The Cruel Sea*?

Round 2
1. Who was the female star of the film *Sleepless in Seattle*?
2. Who partnered Jeremy Bates to victory in the Wimbledon mixed doubles tournament of 1987?
3. Which female aviator flew from Croydon in London to Australia in 19 days in 1930?
4. What was Julius Caesar told to beware of before his assassination?
5. Who was Christine Cagney's partner in the television show *Cagney and Lacey*?

Round 3
1. What word is used to describe a sum of money demanded for the release of a person being held against their will?
2. Who is credited with the invention of frozen food?
3. Which government office was held successively by Geoffrey Howe, Nigel Lawson, and John Major?
4. The first man-made object ever to reach the Moon was a Russian spacecraft which crashed into the Moon in 1959. What was it called?
5. Who was the male presenter of the children's television show *TISWAS*, who also went on to present its adult equivalent, *OTT*?

Game 30 — Rounds 1–3

Round 1
1. Tobias SMOLLETT
2. *Our Man FLINT*
3. HISPANIOLA
4. 'The SILVER Fox'
5. Jack HAWKINS

Quizlink = *Treasure Island* by Robert Louis Stevenson (Smollett was the captain of the schooner *Hispaniola*; that set sail in search of the treasure buried by Captain Flint; Long John Silver was the ship's one-legged cook; and the story was narrated by Jim Hawkins)

Round 2
1. MEG Ryan
2. JO Durie
3. AMY Johnson
4. The Ides of MARCH
5. Mary BETH Lacey

Quizlink = *LITTLE WOMEN* by Louisa May Alcott (the central characters were the four March sisters: Meg; Jo; Amy; and Beth)

Round 3
1. RANSOM
2. Clarence BIRDSEYE
3. CHANCELLOR of the Exchequer
4. LUNA 2
5. Chris TARRANT

Quizlink = *THE BOSTONIANS* by Henry James (Oliver Ransom is a young lawyer who visits Boston on business. He becomes acquainted with Olive Chancellor and her sister Mrs Luna, a widow. Olive takes him to a meeting where he meets Miss Birdseye and Verena Tarrant)

Game 30 — Rounds 4–6

Round 4

1 In which 1963 film starring Doris Day and James Garner does a wife return home after being shipwrecked to discover that her husband has just remarried?
2 Which star of the television show *Eastenders* sang on the 1962 number 1 hit 'Come Outside'?
3 Which Dutch town close to Rotterdam can be reached directly by ferry from the English town of Harwich?
4 Which line follows 'See you later alligator' in the well-known Bill Haley song?
5 What was the title of the theme song used for the film *The Blackboard Jungle*?

Round 5

1 In which North Yorkshire fishing port is there a statue of Captain James Cook overlooking the sea?
2 Which edible bulb of the onion family is composed of small segments called cloves?
3 What title is held by the character Edmund Dantes in a novel by Alexandre Dumas?
4 Which is the highest decoration awarded for bravery by the British armed forces?
5 Which Irish adventurer attempted to steal the British crown jewels in 1671?

Round 6

1 Which television game show is presented by Jim Bowen?
2 What, in a word, are Franciscans, Dominicans, and Cistercians?
3 Who had a 1984 Top 10 hit with the song 'That's Living Alright', the theme tune to the television series *Auf Wiedersehen Pet*?
4 Which US-born woman became, in 1919, the first woman to sit in the House of Commons?
5 Which group had a 1962 number 1 hit with the instrumental 'Nut Rocker'?

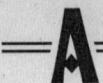

Game 30 — Rounds 4–6

Round 4
1 *Move Over DARLING*
2 WENDY Richards
3 HOOK of Holland
4 'In a while CROCODILE'
5 'Rock Around the CLOCK'

Quizlink = The children's play *Peter Pan* by J M Barrie (Darling is the surname of Wendy and her brothers; Hook is the name of the captain eventually eaten by the crocodile, whose presence was indicated by the ticking of a clock it had swallowed)

Round 5
1 WHITBY
2 GARLIC
3 *The COUNT of Monte Cristo*
4 The Victoria CROSS
5 Colonel Thomas BLOOD

Quizlink = *DRACULA* by Bram Stoker (Whitby was where Count Dracula landed in England; vampires dislike garlic and a cross; but they like blood)

Round 6
1 *BULLSEYE*
2 MONKS
3 Joe FAGIN
4 NANCY Astor
5 B. BUMBLE and the Stingers

Quizlink = *OLIVER TWIST* by Charles Dickens (Bullseye is the name of Bill Sikes's dog; Nancy is his girlfriend; Fagin is the leader of the gang of boy thieves; Bumble is the name of the parish beadle; and Monks turns out to be Oliver's half brother)